When Faith Is All There Is: Faith Is Enough

When Faith Is All There Is: Faith Is Enough

AN ANCIENT PROPHET SPEAKS
TO TODAY'S WORLD

Stanton G. Winder Jr. and Kimberly Allston

Habakkuk Study and Devotional Included

ISBN: 0692987290
ISBN 13: 9780692987292
Library of Congress Control Number: 2017918019
Stanton G. Winder, Ravenel, SC

Dedication

"To my father and mother who taught me the way
of faith and then lived it out every day."
Stanton G. Winder Jr.
"I dedicate this book to my mom who always had faith."
Kimberly Allston

Part One

Is ANYBODY OUT THERE LISTENING? How long, God, must I cry out for help? Where are you? Why do you sit in silence? Why do you stand by while terrorists brutally rape, blow up, behead, and engage in open genocide against your people? Why do criminals receive mercy while the blood of their victims cries out for justice? Why do the rich get richer, while the hard-working poor get poorer? Why does bigotry keep us from unity? Why must a nation founded "under God" be increasingly ruled by jurists that would "legislate" the very mention of God from our public streets? Is justice anywhere to be found? Will you break the silence? Will you right the wrongs? Will you come to our aid?

If you are asking questions like these, you are not alone. Such questions have been asked repeatedly down through the ages. Indeed, if the ancient Hebrew prophet Habakkuk were alive, he would probably be asking the same questions. Unchecked corruption had infiltrated every aspect of his society from the home to the marketplace, from the temple to the palace. Violence, both physical brutality and flaunted moral depravity, had become the new norm. Good and decent people were so outnumbered and overrun by the wicked that the "rule of law was paralyzed and justice perverted" (Habakkuk 1:4). As society unraveled around him, the prophet agonizes, "How long O Lord must I cry for help, but you do not listen?" (1:1; NLT)

Then God breaks the silence, but his answer is frightening, if not downright alarming. Due justice will be done. The wicked will meet their deserved end. The oppressed will be avenged. But all this will happen in a way that the prophet could not possibly have imagined. God's answer is so appalling, so treacherous is the agent of his judgment, that Habakkuk recoils with anger and amazement. How can a holy God use such a vile and unholy nation to slaughter a far less evil nation than they? Isn't this a bit much? Does it not contradict everything about the character of the God that he knows? Where is God's justice?

God's answer is that it will take a journey of faith, a willingness to be patient while God's plan to make all things right, to mete out justice to the unjust, unfolds. "Trust me," says God. "I will make all things right. For the people of God, the best is always yet to come! You've got questions; I've got answers!"

The prophet's story that began with consternation will end with celebration. As one scholar writes, "Habakkuk does not end with a wail, but with a song. It does not end with inquiry, but with affirmation. It does not end with frustration, but with faith." [1]

May I invite you to embark on a journey. It will be a journey much like the prophet before you. What you will discover is that as you grow in your faith (from faith to faith), God will replace your discouragement with encouragement, your perplexities with promises, your consternation with confidence. He can, and will, turn your sorrows into joy.

As we begin our journey, we have divided the book into two parts in order to make this a fruitful endeavor. The first part will primarily engage your mind and the second will speak to your heart. The chapters of *Part One* are meant to introduce, explain and instruct concerning the virtues and character of a life of faith as described in the book of Habakkuk. The devotionals of *Part Two* help you to take what you learn and have it become a source of inspiration, reflection, and day to day practice of this extraordinary life of faith. Together they can be a valuable resource for the classroom, small groups, and individual study. ** **Please note** that the personal Habakkuk Devotion Outline of Part

---

1 Constable, Thomas L. *Notes on Habakkuk.* Sonic Light, 2015. p. 7

Two incorporates the chapters of Part One into four weeks of reflection. This will provide flow and continuity to your study.

Stanton G. Winder Jr.

Part Two

§

WELCOME TO THE HABAKKUK DEVOTION. If you do not know much about Habakkuk, then you are in for a treat. Allow me to introduce you to my favorite male Bible character (besides Jesus) through this devotion.

Habakkuk has become such a strong influence in my life. I've been on a love journey with the book of Habakkuk for a long time. I've studied his life, his words, and his complete resolve to live by faith in difficult circumstances. His story always inspires me to turn my worry into worship and my heartache into hope.

In this personal study of Habakkuk, you will meet a man who gives everything to God. He seeks God and finds Him. He has beautiful conversations with the Lord and turns those conversations into his personal prayers. You too will be inspired to turn Habakkuk's words into personal prayers.

It is a privilege to share my love of Habakkuk with you. It is my prayer that through this man's life, you will find a new voice to converse with our Lord. May God use this study to turn your worry into worship and your heartache into hope.

Kimberly Allston

Part One
Faith's Portrait

§

Stanton G. Winder Jr.

PART ONE
FAITH'S PORTRAIT

Table of Contents

CHAPTER 1
Faith's Honesty (Habakkuk 1:1-4)

∮

IMAGINE RECEIVING A REVELATION so terrifying that you want to sweep it under the carpet, and yet so compelling that you must put pen to paper immediately! Such is this timeless message, this burden, received by the prophet Habakkuk over 2600 years ago. In a dream by night or a vision by day, God had spoken directly to him. And it had all come about because he had dared to confront God, to question his justice, to complain to his face. **He dared to be honest!** He was wearied and worn out by the way things were. It just wasn't right; it just wasn't fair! Habakkuk 1:2-4 (ESV) says:

> *² How long, LORD, must I call for help,*
> *but you do not listen?*
> *Or cry out to you, "Violence!"*
> *but you do not save?*
> *³ Why do you make me look at injustice?*
> *Why do you tolerate wrongdoing?*
> *Destruction and violence are before me;*
> *there is strife, and conflict abounds.*
> *⁴ Therefore the law is paralyzed,*
> *and justice never prevails.*
> *The wicked hem in the righteous,*
> *so that justice is perverted.*

"The prophet is one with all those persons who fervently pray for peace in our world and who experience only war, who pray for God's good to come on earth and who find only human evil. But he is also one with every soul who has prayed for healing beside a sickbed only to be confronted with death; with every spouse who has prayed for love to come into a home and then found only hatred and anger; with every anxious person who has prayed for serenity but then been further disturbed and agitated." [2]

Authentic faith is enough because it begins by being honest. It allows, indeed it drives, you to ask the hard questions. It is open, transparent, seeking and yes demanding answers. The only way to truly trust in God is to search with an insatiable desire to understand his ways and his purposes. *Mature Christian faith is not pretending that we have definitive answers for every question or are denied the ability to ask, "Why?"* Indeed, it was the questioning of God that became the catalyst to the enlarging and assurance of my own faith.

There I sat in the hospital at the foot of the bed staring at the motionless body of my dying father. As I sang his favorite hymns, I prayed that he could hear them. His struggle with strokes and cancer were almost over. I knew that soon an abundant entrance would be granted him into heaven, but O the gnawing grief, the unanswered questions. Why would a gifted professor, pastor, and counselor have suffered so long? Why did one so faithful now lie emaciated, a dying yet living corpse? How was this just? Why would God do this to one of his devoted own?

Habakkuk's questions were my questions. How often have we asked, "God, why aren't you listening? Why the silence? Why do I repeatedly scream for help and there is no response? Is no one home at your address? Rich Mullins in his song, "Hard to Get," describes our frustration:

Do you (Jesus) remember when you lived down here where we all scrape
To find the faith to ask for daily bread?

---

2 C. E. Armerding, "Habakkuk," EBC 7:500.

Did you forget about us after you had flown away?
Well I memorized every word you said.
Still I'm so scared I am holding my breath.
While you are still up there playing hard to get.

To paraphrase Jon Bloom, 'There is meaning in this madness of deprivation. The silence of God intensifies our desire. And the more our desire is heightened, the greater someday its satisfaction will be. Those that mourn will be comforted. The hungry and thirsty will be satisfied. Longing makes us ask. Emptiness makes us seek. Silence makes us knock... But as we will see, God's silence is how it feels, not how it is!'[3]

Habakkuk's first challenge to God is to ask why he has allowed justice in Israel to seemingly become a complete joke. How can the Righteous Judge stand by silently? Why does God let open wickedness go unpunished? This is not the reaction of one who is disloyal to God, but one who is looking for answers to legitimate questions concerning his entrenched faith in God.

Everywhere he looks there is the fruit of injustice. Four unsettling nouns describe the abuses in his society. First, he describes his homeland as experiencing *destruction*, that is decimation and deterioration, the unraveling of its moral and civic fabric as it pursues other gods. His world is also characterized by *unbridled violence*. It is the flaunted moral depravity that rails at God's commandments, and the physical brutality that results from such outright rejection of God's laws. There is no shame, no behavior that is off limits. There is no verbal or physical abuse of the "righteous" or the marginalized and underprivileged that has not been legitimized. All this naturally leads to *strife* and *contention*. "(Such) unchecked wickedness results in

---

3 Jon Bloom, "When God Seems Silent," http://www.desiringgod.org/articles/when-god-seems-silent. July 18, 2014

a divided community riddled with suspicions, accusations, and personal attacks."[4]

The Mosaic and civil laws, Judah's legal system, is "paralyzed" and "perverted" (ESV). Wicked political and religious leaders had made the law of no effect – crooked and perverse. "Habakkuk believed that God's inactivity has caused injustice to become worse. The rich were using their power and money to get what they wanted; the rights of the poor were being trampled on... There was still a righteous remnant, but life was hard for them because they fell prey to the wicked and would not break God's laws to get ahead."[5] Because good people would not circumvent or pervert God's laws, they not only could not get ahead, they became mere onlookers at the collapse of their society.

Does not all of this sound familiar? Our culture is waist-deep in the mud haggling over justice versus injustices. My own home town has become a center for sex trafficking. Then there is illegal verses legal immigration, partial birth abortion, unacceptable poverty rates, the redefining of marriage, true racial discrimination clouded by the constant use of the "race card," the politicization of proper healthcare for all, global warming or no global warming, anarchy and violence in the streets, and free speech legitimizing hate, lewdness, violence, dishonesty, distortions, and every form of depravity on the TV, in the movie houses, and the internet. Injustice is everywhere to be found from the back roads of rural America, to the media, to the halls of government. And yes, it is even found in the American evangelical church, among those who call themselves "Christians."

Indeed, perhaps the best argument against Christianity is the unjust acts of *some* "Christians." (Although, this is certainly not true of many evangelicals.) How often have we seen fellow Christians marginalized, marked by a big stamp on their heads, "not accepted" or made to feel unreasonably uncomfortable. They have committed the "unforgivable"

---

4 Bible Gateway, "Habakkuk 1:3" Reformation Study Bible, 2017
https://www.biblegateway.com/passage/?search=Habakkuk+1%3A3&version=ESV
5 ESV Study Bible, "Habakkuk 1:4," p.1721.

sins of divorce, homosexuality, abortion or drug addictions. Yet their accusers ignore their own struggles with egotism, judgmentalism, gossip, indifference and disregard for the poor. Like the priest and the scribe in the story of the, Good Samaritan (Luke 10:25-37), they hurry on to do their religious duty and fail to see or step over the injured and suffering along the way. As Tim Keller remarks, "Sometimes I look at Christians in society and I wonder if we care more about being right than we do about people… If we are against something it should only be because we are for the people that it is hurting. "[6] Injustice has found its way even into the church of God.

The prophet reminds us that our faith is enough when we begin by daring to be honest with God. The only way to build a relationship is to be vulnerable, to be honest, to reveal our anger and inadequacy. As Rick Warren writes, "Can God handle that kind of frank, intense honesty from you? Absolutely! Genuine friendship is built on disclosure. What may appear as audacity God views as authenticity! God listens to the passionate words of his friends; he is bored with predictable pious clichés. To be God's friend, you must be honest to God, sharing your true feeling."[7] Habakkuk was, will you?

---

6 Tim Keller, "The Church is Responsible for so much Injustice," *Why I'm not a Christian*, Msg.4, http://www.summitrdu.com/wp-content/uploads/sermons/2015/11/2008-09-20_ The-Church-Is-Responsible-For-So-Much-Injustice_Luke-10_25-37.pdf

7 Rick Warren, "Can God Take Your Honesty?" http://www.faithgateway.com/can-god-take-your-honesty/#.WK28w28rLIU

CHAPTER 2
Faith's Humility
(Habakkuk 1:5-17)

§

WE HAVE ALL HEARD IT said, "Be careful what you wish for!" Habakkuk has rightly railed against the violent and unjust wicked who have taken over Judah. Surely God must bring an end to this travesty. Is it not time for some "street justice!" It is! But God's answer will leave him dumbfounded - humbled. It will create a "faith crisis" of epic proportions.

God's answer begins with four sobering directives, "Look...see...wonder...be astounded!" (1:5) Instead of hearing the promise of deliverance and renewal he expected, the prophet hears pronouncements of discipline and retribution. "Just look at the headlines in the media," says God. "Get the global picture! Do you not see Babylon beginning to gobble up the nations around you? [7] Do you not wonder? Do you not marvel that they are headed directly toward you? I have not been sitting idly by. *Brace yourself for a shock! Something's about to take place and you're going to find it hard to believe* (The Message, 1:5). I will use the violence of Babylon to judge the violence in Judah. I will do the unthinkable, the unbelievable in bringing about justice! I can because of who I am. I am sovereign over and ever involved in the affairs of the nations!"[7]

---

7 Most scholars believe the prophet wrote sometime between 609 and 598 B. C. (See Patterson on Habakkuk in the Wycliffe Exegetical Commentary, p. 115.) This would mean that the prophet would have lived through the time when Babylon defeated the Assyrian Empire, the Egyptians, and possibly the first of three deportations of Jewish captives in 605 B. C.

What comes next is a vivid description of this coming **"face of evil."**

For behold, I am raising up the Chaldeans,
that bitter and hasty nation,
who march through the breadth of the earth,
to seize dwellings not their own.
⁷ They are dreaded and fearsome;
their justice and dignity go forth from themselves.
⁸ Their horses are swifter than leopards,
more fierce than the evening wolves;
their horsemen press proudly on.
Their horsemen come from afar;
they fly like an eagle swift to devour.
⁹ They all come for violence,
all their faces forward.
They gather captives like sand.
¹⁰ At kings they scoff,
and at rulers they laugh.
They laugh at every fortress,
for they pile up earth and take it.
¹¹ Then they sweep by like the wind and go on,
guilty men, whose own might is their god!" (1: 6-11;ESV)

Faith in this life will constantly be challenged by the menace of evil. What is interesting is that the face of evil never changes. It was then as it is now. And what does this monster evil look like? This passage paints a striking picture! First, *evil is always "on the take."* It has a voracious appetite driven by unbridled greed. Evil will rob you of your freedom, your wealth, and ultimately your health. The Babylonians marched through the Mideast enriching themselves with that which was not their own. It is one thing to acquire wealth through fair trade, but quite another through seizing it.

The face of evil is marked by a profound dissatisfaction with what you are and what you have. And that malcontent will not stop at anything including robbing others of their life, liberty, relationships, employment or possessions. As psychologist Erich Fromm writes in *Escape from Freedom*, "Greed is a bottomless pit which exhausts the person in an endless effort to satisfy the need without ever reaching satisfaction."[8]

Second, *evil is a law unto itself*. Evil people and evil nations make up and write their own rulebook as they go. They stand defiantly against any court and any government. They pillage and butcher at their own discretion. The New American Commentary says of Babylon, "Such people acknowledge no accountability, seek no repentance, and offer no reparations, while violating the most fundamental order of created life."[9] And when this arrogance and lawlessness is wed with power, it brings terror to all who lie in their path. No better example can be given than the abuse of the present-day government of North Korea toward its citizens. This is a state that carries out public executions even in school yards. The *Human Rights Watch World Report 2017* chronicles these abuses stating that "systematic, widespread, and gross human rights violations committed by the government included murder, enslavement, torture, imprisonment, rape, forced abortion, and other sexual violence, and constituted crimes against humanity." Somewhere between 80-100,000 citizens are interned in detention camps and the majority in North Korea experience some form of daily mandatory government labor.[10] North Korea has become a law unto itself, flaunting its deplorable acts in the face of the nations and threatening a nuclear holocaust.

Third, *the face of evil is the face of unstoppable violence*. Babylon was the preeminent world power in Habakkuk's day. Indeed, its power was its "god." The prophet uses vivid imagery to describe their military prowess (the swiftness of a leopard, the dive of the eagle, the vicious attack

---

8 Erich Fromm." BrainyQuote.com. Xplore Inc, 2017. 19 April 2017. https://www. brainyquote.com/quotes/quotes/e/erichfromm391095.htm
9 Barker, Kenneth L., and Waylon Bailey. *Micah, Nahum, Habakkuk, Zephaniah*, p. 344.
10 https://www.hrw.org/world-report/2017/country-chapters/north-korea

by a pack of wolves at dusk). Their cavalry moved quickly across the landscape like the winds of a thunderstorm or Hitler's panzer divisions in WWII - devouring a whole country in a couple of weeks or months. Like cruise missiles, they seemed to come out of nowhere swooping down and leaving nothing but carnage and destruction in their wake. They gathered up the best and the brightest by the hundreds and thousands. Like the hot dry Sirocco winds from the east they "piled up the desert sand" moving quickly on from one country to the next. You can hear them scoff and laugh as they wall up the rubble from one city to overcome the fortifications of the next.

What then are we to say in the face of such evil? What are we to say of the ravenous appetite among many today driven by the lust for more at the expense of their families, friends and society around them? What are we to say when leaders and professors condone, if not foment, acts of violence while making excuses for every imaginable evil? What are we to say when increasingly a vortex of violence is dragging our nations downward endangering the very livelihood of our civilization. Is God again allowing a strange instrument like Islamic terrorists, North Korea or Iran to bring the world to its knees in order that He might lift it up, in order that He might revive and renew it again? Perhaps!

In the face of this evil, Habakkuk recoils in fear and shock, if not disgust. This could not possibly be the answer from God that he was looking for! How could God use such a monster to be the agent of judgment and discipline upon these sinful Judeans? Hear it in the prophet's own words:

> [12] *Are you not from everlasting,*
> *O LORD my God, my Holy One?*
> *We shall not die.*
> *O LORD, you have ordained them as a judgment,*
> *and you, O Rock, have established them for reproof.*
> [13] *You who are of purer eyes than to see evil*
> *and cannot look at wrong,*

> *why do you idly look at traitors*
> *and remain silent when the wicked swallows up*
> *the man more righteous than he?*
> *¹⁴ You make mankind like the fish of the sea,*
> *like crawling things that have no ruler.*
> *¹⁵ He brings all of them up with a hook;*
> *he drags them out with his net;*
> *he gathers them in his dragnet;*
> *so he rejoices and is glad.*
> *¹⁶ Therefore he sacrifices to his net*
> *and makes offerings to his dragnet;*
> *for by them he lives in luxury,*
> *and his food is rich.*
> *¹⁷ Is he then to keep on emptying his net*
> *and mercilessly killing nations forever? (1: 12-17; ESV)*

Surprisingly, the prophet's first words, his first reaction to this malevolent nemesis, are an expression of a confident mature faith in the nature of his God. "My God" is eternal. He is the God who has always been and always will be (Psalm 90:2). Consequently, he is the God of history, the God of the Exodus who delivered his people from slavery in Egypt (Exodus 6: 2-8). He is Yahweh, the great "I AM" (Exodus 3:14)! That is, he is utterly independent (self- existing – has and draws life from himself, self-sustaining, self-determining) in need of no thing and no one. As such the prophet sees God, in the words of J. I. Packer, as "the living, reigning, potent, unfettered and undiminished king." He is sovereign over the affairs of this world.[11] He is holy, totally separate from and intolerant of all forms of sin. His eyes cannot "wink" at or allow sin to go unchecked. He is the Rock, a firm foundation guaranteeing security and stability in the time of crisis and trial.

In light of all this, Judah cannot and will not be vanquished from the earth. God must remain faithful to his promises made to Abraham,

---

11 J. I. Packer, *Knowing God*, p. 24.

to Moses, and to David. God has forever been the protector and deliverer of his people. He most certainly will preserve a believing remnant. Why? Because the agent of punishment or correction (Babylon) is under the hand of God whose ultimate goal is restoration, not annihilation.

All this being so, yet incredulity and perplexity follow. Does what he believes correspond to reality? Are not the evils of Babylon far greater than the failings of Judah? How can God overlook, how can His holy mind and heart stomach the violence and wickedness of Judah's oppressors? How can He "remain silent when the wicked swallows up the man more righteous than he?" (ESV, verse 13). Does this not contradict the justice, even the character of the God Habakkuk knows? Will he not become responsible for the fate of Babylon's victims? If he cannot even look upon evil, then how can he use the vilest of the vile to be his agents of judgement upon his own people? Is God out of kilter, engaged in a full-blown temper tantrum?

What's more, "had the Creator now forgotten his creatures? Had the powerful Babylonians become so powerful they exercised control over what God created?"[12] Had they become "God" in their own right? Certainly, they thought so! Can such divine behavior further the coming of God's kingdom? Is God replacing a backslidden nation who has "gone to the dogs" with the rule of a foreign people or peoples who will forever prevent the advent of God's glorious reign on the earth?

"Look around," says the prophet. "Are the nations of the earth as powerless as fish squirming as they are herded into the Babylonian net? Are they strung up like fish on a line? Indeed, Babylonian monuments depicted the Chaldeans as driving a hook through the lower lip of their captives and stringing them single file, like fish on a line.[13] Must Babylon go on making sacrifices to these "nets," worshipping the military might that has made them rich. Further, will this ever end? Will these evil oppressors keep filling and emptying their nets?

---

12 Ibid, Barker and Bailey, p. 348.
13 W. Rudolph, *Micha-Nahum-Habakuk-Zephanja*, p. 211.

Authentic faith will often be challenged and humbled by the face of evil. God uses the furnaces and agents of affliction to purge the pride and failures of his people. Suffering will remove all remnants of self-reliance and worship that can only lead to our undoing. We must ever remember that Judah was in a dire straight because of their own compulsion of doing things their own way. When God is forced to the perimeter of our lives, then the blessings of intimacy and friendship with God subsequently begin to disappear from our lives. If God is love, then to live deliberately in rebellion against God is to partner with a society filled with the opposite of love - indifference, hatred, abuse, and isolation. Is that the world we want? It will surely be the world we get!

What a contrast to the unconditional, compassionate, non-discriminating world of God's people living in the fellowship of God's love! Evil in all its forms, expressions, and resultant outcomes establishes, clashes with, reveals the profoundly opposite character of God. As Carson states, "evil is evil because it is rebellion against God...the ugliness of evil is established (revealed) by the beauty of God; the filth of evil is established (revealed) by the purity of God; the selfishness of evil is established (revealed) by the love of God."[14] God uses the furnaces of affliction and discipline to show us how sad and silly it is to live a life with God in the margins or a life lived in direct opposition to a life with God.

Accordingly, we are also reminded that our perspective is often in sharp contrast to God's perspective. We look for the punishment of the wicked so that the prosperity of God's people might be assured. But God, who knows the end from the beginning, often sees that the discipline of God's people through these "evil agents" is essential to their restoration to God.[15] When we are humbled, when we are brought down, then in contrition and repentance we can experience the joy of ascending - the journey back up and beyond. To paraphrase John

14 D. A. Carson, *How Long O Lord*, p. 42.
15 Barber, Habakkuk and Zephaniah, p. 36.

Maxwell, 'It is our perspective, not necessarily the problem, that needs to change.'

Jon Bloom aptly writes: "We are often unprepared for the answers we receive from God. His answers frequently do not look at first like answers. They look like problems. They look like trouble. They look like loss, disappointment, affliction, conflict, sorrow, and increased selfishness. They cause deep soul wrestling and expose sin and doubts and fears. They are not what we expect, and we often do not see how they correspond to our prayers."[15] Habakkuk surely didn't, but he will! And we too will learn that painful humiliation and suffering are often wedded to the enlargement and to the electrifying ultimate triumph of our faith.

---

16 Jon Bloom, http://www.desiringgod.org/articles/the-unexpected-answers-of-god, July 11, 2014.

CHAPTER 3

Faith's Perseverance (Habakkuk 2:1-5)

§

How OFTEN HAVE YOU HEARD the phrase, "wait for it…wait for it" as someone tries to build suspense for what they seem to think is important or a climatic event. Faith is much more than checking off a list of doctrines on a statement or creed. Let's see, "I believe in one God, the Father Almighty, maker of heaven and earth." Check! "I believe in one Lord, Jesus Christ, the only Son of God. Check! Further, it is more than a simple prayer to receive Christ as Savior. There is no doubt that the Nicene Creed may be the greatest short summary of the Christian faith ever written. And one cannot overstate the absolute necessity of trusting in Christ alone to deliver us from our sin and make us fit for heaven. But assent to the truth is much different from a dogged persistence in living out these truths in our lives. Salvation is not merely a point in time; it is a process through time. "The just SHALL LIVE by faith" (2:4). Faith is a lifestyle – an unwavering trust in God when the day is bright and also in the darkest days when you feel betrayed and forgotten – when you must wait, "wait for it."

Chapter two begins with these words (2:1-5 ESV)

I will take my stand at my watchpost
and station myself on the tower,
and look out to see what he will say to me,

and what I will answer concerning my complaint.
[2] And the LORD answered me:
"Write the vision;
make it plain on tablets,
so he may run who reads it.
[3] For still the vision awaits its appointed time;
it hastens to the end—it will not lie.
If it seems slow, wait for it;
it will surely come; it will not delay.
Behold, his soul is puffed up; it is not upright within him,
but the righteous shall live by his faith.
[5] Moreover, wine is a traitor,
an arrogant man who is never at rest
His greed is as wide as Sheol;
like death he has never enough.
He gathers for himself all nations
and collects as his own all peoples.

Habakkuk has two choices: "He can allow his doubts to be destructive or creative. He can use his doubts, struggles, and agonizing questions to turn from God and to renounce his faith. Or he can keep his hold on God, trusting him for an answer."[87] He can protest and walk away or he can persevere and wait.

But what does it mean to "wait for it?" *First, it means to be daily on the lookout with an ongoing commitment to watch for God to answer.* It does little good to ask questions that only God can answer and then pursue the answer elsewhere. Notice how the prophet stations himself on the tower away from the business of city life. Here he can give full attention, free from distraction, to the voice of God. And so it is with us! We must set apart time away from the hustle and bustle of modern day life if we are to clearly hear and receive God's answers. Perhaps the reason for the common complaint that God is distant from us is because we

---

17 Heflin, Nahum, Habakkuk, Zephaniah, and Haggai, p. 87.

have made ourselves distant from him. Prayer and daily time spent in the Scriptures have become an anomaly rather than a passion for many followers of Christ. You can't receive a revelation if you don't watch for a revelation. You can't receive an answer if you are not diligently seeking an answer.

Second, it means humble submission and faith in God's timing. This is where it gets really hard. In a day where we want instant everything, it is seemingly impossible to wait. And indeed, you will not wait, unless you believe: 1) that only God can unravel the perplexities and mysteries both of his dealings broadly in the world and more narrowly in your own personal life; 2) that God's timing, not your timing, is everything! It takes time for you to emotionally and spiritually, if not intellectually, get to the place where you can both receive and accept God's answers. It takes time alone, talking and listening to God, to come to an assured conviction that God only does what is best for you and your future. It takes time for God to work in your life and the lives of others – to unfold his plan and to work out the circumstances of that plan. It takes time! And when the right moment, the appointed time comes, God will reveal all that you need to know.

Third, it means patience knowing that God will surely answer. The prophet is certain that even if God's answer "seems slow," God will answer. His perseverance will be rewarded. So confident is he, that he's already deliberating as to his responses. Is that not like us. We often ask questions and answer our questions ahead of time. We then wait or expect God to agree with us. And we make sure that we are ready with a preponderance of arguments in case we don't get the answer we like. But the important thing here is both the certainty of an answer and God's gracious willingness to dialogue with us. God knows that both his answer and the ensuing conversation can be a very positive growing experience for us.

Fourth, what we wait for can be trusted. Life experiences tell us a quick answer is not often a trustworthy answer. The prophet is assured, as can we be assured, that when God's answer comes it will be free from any falsehood. God does not and cannot lie (Hebrews 6:18). Further, since God's knowledge of the future is exhaustive and his power to do his own holy will is unlimited, his predictions will come to fruition. God will make all things right. He will avenge the evil actions of the enemies of his people. The fulfillment of God's message is sure! This necessitates proclaiming it far and wide. Like a billboard sign along the highway or an ad on Facebook, the message must be made plain and clear for all passing by to understand. Trustworthy messages demand trustworthy messengers.

Fifth, our patient perseverant trust is a lifestyle. Our whole lives can be captioned as those who "wait for it." As the ESV Study Bible (p.1724) states, "The kind of faith that Habakkuk describes, and that the NT writers promote, is continuing trust in God, and clinging to God's promises, even in the darkest days." Such trust in God provides moral and spiritual stability. They, the trusting, are by their faith made trustworthy. They, and the message they proclaim, can be counted on in a world where little seems worthy of being counted upon.

Finally, one cannot escape the contrast between those who "wait for it" (the righteous) and those who don't (the unrighteous). It is a contrast between those who trust in God and those who trust in themselves. The unrighteous nation of Babylon, as well as its king, is described as "puffed up, not upright and arrogant." Those who trust in themselves are by nature "ballooning" with pride and self-absorption. Whether it be their military power, wealth, education, intellect or pedigree, they have no need of anyone but themselves. They refuse to be reined in by any moral rectitude. Like those who are intoxicated, they are deceived by a false view of reality. They pursue what they believe to be an abundant life, but what will, in the end, prove only to be death. The "handwriting is on the wall" and they do not even know it. They are restless, never able to be satisfied with what they have, but always driven by a voracious appetite to pillage everyone and thing around them for more. As the *Message* states (speaking of Babylon),

> *They are more hungry for wealth*
> *than the grave is for cadavers.*
> *Like death, they always want more,*
> *but the 'more' they get is dead bodies.*
> *They are cemeteries filled with dead nations,*
> *graveyards filled with corpses.* (2:5)

The gauntlet is about to fall. The axe is laid at the root. And like many today, they do not even see their judgment coming.

What are you waiting for? The prophet was waiting for things to be made right. What wrong are you waiting to be made right? Are you still waiting to hear the words, "I'm sorry" from a spouse, a parent, a friend or a relative? Are you waiting for property to be returned that was so egregiously taken from you? Are you waiting for a long-deserved promotion or an increase in your pay check? Are you waiting for a "prodigal" or a "missing person" to return home? Or perhaps you are waiting to "crossover" to be with someone who prematurely was taken from this life. For what are you called to persevere, to "wait for it."

Remember those moments I spent by my Dad's bedside as he lay in the throes and agony of death – a seemingly endless struggle with suffering, with "waiting for it?" How did my mom, my family, myself go on? How did we persevere? First, we knew that Dad would soon step into his heavenly home. What hope! There Dad would never again feel the grip of searing physical pain consuming his body. He would never experience again the pain of fear, betrayal, being misunderstood, grief or failure. Nothing but boundless joy and inestimable love lay ahead for him. Second, we knew the amazing grace of God our Savior would reunite us at our death or at that great meeting in the air. Third, in the midst of our grief, we received an unexplainable supernatural peace which strengthened and compelled us to go on. All those verses Dad had taught us ran like a movie through our heads. Here are just a few of them:

> *Do not let your hearts be troubled. You believe in God; believe also in me. My Father's house has many rooms; if that were not so, would I have told you that I am going there to prepare a place for you? And if I go and prepare a place for you, I will come back and take you to be with me that you also may be where I am… Peace I leave with you; my peace I give you. I do not give to you as the world gives. Do not let your hearts be troubled and do not be afraid (John 14:1-3, 27 NIV).*

CHAPTER 4

Faith's Revenge
(Habakkuk 2:6-20)

§

I CAN STILL HEAR THE mournful wail of the *Hee-Haw* TV show lyrics: "Doom, despair and agony on me. Deep dark depression, excessive misery…" Such will be the end for the invincible, the unassailable Babylon. In the face of this military giant are pronounced five scorn-filled taunts of woe. The oppressor will be oppressed. The dam will break and the fury of God's vengeance will obliterate this great empire from the pages of history. Her doom and destruction are sure! Justice may be delayed, but it will surely not be denied.

To the people of God, then and now, comes the promise of faith's "revenge". We will see the enemies of God overturned. They will be brought to justice. God sees their acts of brutality. He hears their words of disdain and ridicule against the people of God and the commandments of God. They who believe themselves to be wise will be proven to be utterly foolish. They who propagate their wicked ways throughout the earth will be removed from the earth to their rightful end. "Vengeance is mine says the Lord, I will repay!" (Deuteronomy 32:35; Romans 12:19) Rest comfortably, patiently, God assures us, leave it to me. I will avenge the righteous; I will make all things right! I cannot be stopped and my justice shall not be declared unjust.

The five woes against Babylon are five indictments against Babylon and indeed all the enemies of God: The wicked plunder (2: 6-8); the wicked plot (2: 9-11); the wicked perpetrate violence (2: 12-14); the wicked pronounce shame (2: 15-17); and the wicked promote idolatry (2:18-20). *But equally important, the wicked will get their just due. Those who plunder will be plundered. Those who have plotted the ruin of others will themselves be ruined. Those who perpetuate violence will be the recipients of violence. Those who heap shame will bring shame to themselves. Those who trust in idols will find their trust betrayed.* The road ahead for them is a road ending in demise and disaster.

But the question that still haunts the prophet is, "How long?" How long until the people of God are avenged? (2:6, cf. 1:2). It is a question that for a time will go unanswered. It is a question that still arises in our minds today as we are also confronted with grotesque and gruesome forms of evil. How long, Lord?

This entreaty is especially meaningful as we now consider these well-deserved incriminations against the evil of Habakkuk's day and its grim representations in our day. First, the wicked plunder (2:6-8). They are consumed with ill-gotten gain.

> *⁶ Shall not all these take up their taunt against him,*
> *with scoffing and riddles for him, and say,*
> *"Woe to him who heaps up what is not his own -*
> *for how long? -*
> *and loads himself with pledges!"*
> *⁷ Will not your debtors suddenly arise,*
> *and those awake who will make you tremble?*
> *Then you will be spoil for them.*
> *⁸ Because you have plundered many nations,*
> *all the remnant of the peoples shall plunder you,*
> *for the blood of man and violence to the earth,*
> *to cities and all who dwell in them.*

Babylon pillaged, flat out robbed and economically raped its conquered nations. They amassed great wealth by extortion through accumulation of (so-called) 'pledges' (RSV; NEB; JB; cf. Deut. 24:10–13). These were items supposed to be used as security (or collateral) in case of default on a loan. But they, too often, were confiscated prematurely or without thought for the needs of the borrower.[18] The Babylonians seized the pledges of its victims (conquered peoples) and either kept the pledges or made the victims pay what they did not owe.[19]

This abomination has not escaped the all-seeing eyes of God. What goes around will come around. We reap what we sow {Galatians 6:7). Often what we do will come back to haunt us in some form of poetic justice. And, so it is with Babylon! They who have extorted will be extorted. They who have plundered and pillaged will be plundered and pillaged. They who have murdered and massacred will be decimated by the incoming armies of the Medes and Persians (in 539 B. C.).

Let this be a lesson to us! God certainly rewards hard work and legitimate profit margins. But he does not look kindly upon exorbitant interest rates or amassing wealth at the expense of the poor or the working class. At the final judgment, our greatness will be defined by our benevolence not our economic prosperity (Matthew 25: 34-40). I believe history will look kindly upon those moments when Americans' largesse evidenced itself in rebuilding the infrastructure of Germany and Japan after WWII, American aid after the 2010 Haiti earthquake, and the 2004 tsunami in the Indian Ocean. May we ever be a beacon of hope to those who flee religious persecution and economic oppression.

Second, the wicked plot (2: 9-11). Whereas the preceding verses emphasize the "crime" itself, now the crime is reiterated, but the motive behind it is also unveiled. It is all about maintaining security. *The Message* conveys the thought well:

Who do you think you are-
recklessly grabbing and looting,
Living it up, acting like king of the mountain,

---

18 David Baker, *Nahum, Habakkuk, Zephaniah*, p.51
19 Barker, Kenneth L., and Waylon Bailey. *Micah, Nahum, Habakkuk, Zephaniah*, p. 382.

> *acting above it all, above trials and troubles?*
> *You've engineered the ruin of your own house.*
> *In ruining others you've ruined yourself.*
> *You've undermined your foundations,*
> *rotted out your own soul.*
> *The bricks of your house will speak up and accuse you.*
> *The woodwork will step forward with evidence.*

Their unjust evil gain was meant to, like the eagle's nest, place the palace and the kingdom high above and far beyond any possibility of harm or ruin. They had found safety, they thought, in their economic and military superiority. No trial, no trouble, no power could bring them down. Indeed, this is why the king of Babylon would "party on" even while the enemy stood outside his gates (Daniel 5). In his mind, the city was invincible and impervious to all danger. The historian, Herodotus, spoke of its one hundred bronze gates and massive walls atop which a four-horse chariot could race (*History* 1.178-79). Apparently, the king was not the only one who thought Babylon to be invincible!

Certainly, the reality was far different from their prideful perception! Saving for a rainy day is wise and rewarding. A strong military is a helpful deterrent. But there was one fatal flaw – their pride. They believed that they could plot against and pillage others without retribution. They were wrong! Not only were they shamed in the eyes of the peoples they had ground to dust, but God would bring shame by grinding them into dust. Their disregard for the shedding of innocent blood would ultimately lead to the shedding of their own blood. As testimony to the rightness of God's judgement, the stone, gold, silver and building materials, taken from other nation's buildings in constructing their own, now stood as a "monument," a continual visual reminder, to the treachery of these acts.

Third, the wicked perpetrate violence (2: 12-14). We have all heard of "blood money." It was the spoils of war obtained through bloodshed and the blood and sweat of forced labor that fueled Nebuchadnezzar's massive building projects (i.e., numerous ornate temples, the Hanging Gardens of Babylon and the Ishtar Gate). It was an empire and a city built on unjust acts. God would have nothing of it! And soon all these attempts at self-aggrandizement and self-glory would go up in flames. In but a few decades, this great empire came crashing down demonstrating the temporality and futility of man's glory - "Babylon's glory." Listen to the prophet's words:

> *12 Woe to him who builds a town with blood*
> *and founds a city on iniquity!*
> *13 Behold, is it not from the LORD of hosts*
> *that peoples labor merely for fire,*
> *and nations weary themselves for nothing?*
> *14 For the earth will be filled*
> *with the knowledge of the glory of the LORD*
> *as the waters cover the sea.*

In sharp contrast, the prophet speaks of a coming day when God's glory will fill the whole earth. God will wonderfully and recognizably be present, and the knowledge of him will be as deep and wide as the oceans (Numbers 14:21; Ps 72:19; Isa 6:3). In contrast to the violence of Babylon it will be a time when the whole universe will be a sanctuary of peace - freed from the moral and physical pollution of sin and pure and pristine in every way. The lion will lay down with the lamb, the leopard and goat will be at peace, and our cats will frolic with our dogs.

As our world travails under the weight of terrorists' bombings snuffing out the life of children and infants, as the sex traffic industry enslaves millions across the globe, as the Coptic church martyrs, and many others, cry for the avenging on their ISIS killers, we too long for that day when we will study war no more. The stain of blood money is to be found everywhere, but a new day is coming!

Fourth, the wicked pronounce shame (2:15-17). They live to embarrass, to disgrace, to discredit others.

> ¹⁵ *Woe to him who makes his neighbors drink—*
> *you pour out your wrath and make them drunk,*
> *in order to gaze at their nakedness!*
> ¹⁶ *You will have your full of shame instead of glory.*
> *Drink, yourself, and show your uncircumcision!*
> *The cup in the LORD's right hand*
> *will come around to you,*
> *and utter shame will come upon your glory!*
> ¹⁷ *The violence done to Lebanon will overwhelm you,*
> *as will the destruction of the beasts that terrified them,*
> *for the blood of man and violence to the earth,*
> *to cities and all who dwell in them.*

We are all familiar with the consequences of drunken parties. We have seen or heard how they incapacitate, confuse, and dupe minds. We have witnessed the humiliation brought when alcohol breaks down inhibitions and leaves its victims "naked" and vulnerable. Babylon was known for such drunken orgies and at times using them for the purpose of manipulating, exposing, and disgracing others. The very night the empire fell, such a travesty enveloped the palace. During the party, the king called for the stolen drinking vessels from the Jewish temple, sacred vessels set apart for worship! Imagine how profane and shameful this must have been to the Jewish people. Imagine using the Eucharistic or Seder cup today for such a purpose.

This is just one way in which Babylon took shameful (at times even sexual) advantage of their conquered peoples. It also seems the prophet is using this picture figuratively, illustrating how Babylon would force the subdued nations to drink from the cup of their wrath (military campaigns) and then rape them of all they had. As an example, the Babylonians stripped the forests of Lebanon of their grand giant cedars for their ambitious building projects and, as a consequence, the shelter they gave for wild animals. Further, it seems that they too, like the Assyrians, engaged in grandiose hunting expeditions there.[20]

God's response is furious and frightening! They were about to drink a cup of judgement which would so utterly destroy and disgrace them, that never again would they reign as a world power in history. They who have uncovered the nakedness of others are about to have (as the Hebrew reads in graphic language) their own genitals exposed. Exposing the sexual organs would mean a double disgrace and judgement as they would be shown to be uncircumcised – outside of the people and blessing of God.[21] They whose myopic focus was on self-honor (self-glory) are now utterly devoid of honor. They who have done violence to God's creation and God's people are now the subjects of God' violence and degradation.

There is much for us to learn here. For one thing, we live in a culture where shaming and disgracing others is acceptable, where impugning motives, destroying reputations is often the feverish intent of the daily news. Where once a degree of civility and propriety was expected in journalism, there is now endless room for crude, vulgar, hateful, even inciting verbiage. Making news has replaced reporting news. What we hear is "fake news, hate news" instead of "straight news." And the antidote is not simply changing the channel. Embarrassing and discrediting others has woven its way into the whole of our society.

What is worse is that this is seen as innocuous when such speech is tearing at the very fabric of our individual as well as communal relationships. As Psychology Today warns, "shaming others often becomes the root of depression, anxiety, unsafe sex, and eating disorders. Feelings of shame feed a toxic emotional and psychological mix that includes a sense of worthlessness and powerlessness...a sense of shrinking and of being small." They go on to speak of aggressive behaviors

---

20 ESV Study Bible, p. 1725.
21 Barker, Kenneth L., and Waylon Bailey. *Micah, Nahum, Habakkuk, Zephaniah*, p. 393.

and of paralyzing guilt complexes.[22] This is serious business! It destroys not only the body, but the soul. Verbal violence can be as destructive as physical violence.

One more thing is God's attitude toward our care for his creation. We as Christians are stewards of the environment. The unnecessary pollution or destruction of any of our natural resources is an affront to God. Babylon's destruction of Lebanon's forests would impact the land, animals and human population for centuries. As one scholar writes, "It is one thing to rule over creation, respecting it as God's creation entrusted to one for the moment (cf. Deut 22:6-7; 25:4; Prov 12:10; 27:23); it is quite another thing to exploit it unmercifully as though it belonged to one absolutely, as though one were not accountable for it to its creator."[23] We need to spend as much time caring for the wondrous gift of nature bestowed upon us as we do wrangling over (mounting our arguments for or against) global warming.

Fifth, the wicked promote the folly of idolatry. Habakkuk writes:

> [18] *"What profit is an idol*
> *when its maker has shaped it,*
> *a metal image, a teacher of lies?*
> *For its maker trusts in his own creation*
> *when he makes speechless idols!*
> [19] *Woe to him who says to a wooden thing, Awake;*
> *to a silent stone, Arise!*
> *Can this teach?*
> *Behold, it is overlaid with gold and silver,*
> *and there is no breath at all in it.*
> [20] *But the LORD is in his holy temple;*
> *let all the earth keep silence before him."*

---

22 https://www.psychologytoday.com/blog/living-single/201506/11-reasons-never-shame-anyone

23 Roberts, Nahum, Habakkuk, and Zephaniah, p. 125.

One of the most senseless and futile things in the world is to worship that which you can create with your hands or fully image with your own mind. If you can fashion it or imagine it, then it is no greater than you are. No matter what your material idol looks like or what it is made of, it is a non-entity, it doesn't really exist. The idols of Babylon looked great on the outside but were lifeless on the inside. Consequently, it was utter nonsense to expect them to instruct, to react to or to answer any entreaty. As Baker states, "Instead of finding a source for truth, one who approaches idols finds a 'teacher' of lies (cf. Isa. 9:15), something that not only does not perform its intended function, but in fact leads its worshippers into error by leading them away from the true and self-revealing God (cf. 1 Cor. 12:2)."[24]

In sharp contrast to these silent speechless idols is the awesome God of the universe. Over against their inability to speak is his sovereign power to silence all of creation before him. Over against their inability to advise or instruct is his infinite wisdom to guide, answer, comfort and astound. Over against their non-existence he sits forever enthroned in his heavenly temple. Over against their lies he is holy and pure, the source of truth and the disseminator of truth. He is Lord of lords - the only true God.

What then are the idols that we prostrate ourselves before? What are the idols that we fashion with our hands or envision in our minds? An idol is anything we place ahead of or above the one true God. It can be a spouse, a child, a career, a car, a creation, a bank account, an obsessive fantasy, gaming, a stock portfolio, a business or anything else that we adore, trust in, rely on or put in the place of God. Indeed, quite often it is a "good thing" that becomes our idol – the enemy of the best. But when we finally believe, passionately believe, that God only and always wants what is best for us, these idols and the "woes" they bring disappear from our lives.

And now we have come to the summary of the matter. We have heard God's answer to Habakkuk's question. God will take care of

---

24 Baker, p. 56-57

the adversary of God's people. He will show that the gods of Babylon (chiefly Bel and Nebo) are impotent. When the Babylonians cry to them for help before the armies of the Medes and Persians, there will be nothing but eerie silence, endless woe, and futile desperation. In his own time and his own way, God will avenge the enemies of his people.

CHAPTER 5
Faith's Hope (Habakkuk 3:1-19)

§

HAVE YOU NOT HEARD IT said that "hope springs eternal" when confronted by the thunder clouds of adversity?[25] When the devoted Christ follower runs into a brick wall, how often I have seen him or her respond with the words of a song – a hymn of praise, a song of victory. How can that be! What anchors them? What stabilizes them? We find the answer in the prayer sung by the prophet Habakkuk.

I have heard of your fame; I stand in awe of your deeds (3:2a, *NIV*). From a child up, he had heard the stories of the plagues in Egypt, the parting of the Red Sea, the food from heaven, the water from a rock, and the covenant made at Mount Sinai with God's people Israel. If God had rescued them from slavery then, would he not rescue them in the foreboding future? Even as his knees doubled under and a panic attack threatened at his heart's door, He was steadied by a sense of awe and wonder.

He would stop only for a moment to petition before his song erupted with visions of the power, the grandeur, and the mercy and grace of God. O Lord in this time of great need, *do among us what you did among them. Work among us what you worked among them. And as you bring judgment...remember mercy*, (3:2b, *The Message*). Based upon God's deliverance of Israel in the past, there was and could be hope for the future.

Is this not our prayer? O, Lord, bring life, "revive us," remind us of the wonder and awe of God's presence among your people in the past.

---

25 From Alexander Pope's *Essay on Man*.

Give us a fresh new vision of your glory and grandeur. Fill our hearts with your love. May our souls be rekindled with fire from above. And as your "holy fire" disciplines us and corrects us for our chronic waywardness, remember the tenderness and gentleness of your mercy.

The prophet's psalm (song) begins with God coming, God appearing, God showing up big time! It is what theologians call a theophany – an event where God appears in a striking way with great power, splendor and glory. Such "comings" are the basis of faith's hope. God *has come* in his appearances during the Exodus from Egypt, the incarnation (God in human flesh) in the person of Jesus Christ, and the descent of the Holy Spirit at Pentecost. God *will come* in the climatic event of Christ's Second Coming at the end of history. God has come and will come!

As Habakkuk revisits Israel's salvation route in the past, it portends the final deliverance of God's people in the future. In the regions of Teman and Mount Paran, Israel had seen God in full display at Mt. Sinai as He lead them through the desert with a cloud by day and a pillar of fire by night (See Deuteronomy 33:2-4). It is God's powerful person and presence in history that will now frame the prophet's hope.

³ God came from Teman,
and the Holy One from Mount Paran. Selah
His splendor covered the heavens,
and the earth was full of his praise.
⁴ His brightness was like the light;
rays flashed from his hand;
and there he veiled his power.
⁵ Before him went pestilence,
and plague followed at his heels.
⁶ He stood and measured the earth;
he looked and shook the nations;
then the eternal mountains were scattered;
the everlasting hills sank low.
His were the everlasting ways.

> ⁷ *I saw the tents of Cushan in affliction;*
> *the curtains of the land of Midian did tremble.*
> ⁸ *Was your wrath against the rivers, O* LORD?
> *Was your anger against the rivers,*
> *or your indignation against the sea,*
> *when you rode on your horses,*
> *on your chariot of salvation?*
> ⁹ *You stripped the sheath from your bow,*
> *calling for many arrows. Selah*
> *You split the earth with rivers.*
> ¹⁰ *The mountains saw you and writhed;*
> *the raging waters swept on;*
> *the deep gave forth its voice;*
> *it lifted its hands on high.*
> ¹¹ *The sun and moon stood still in their place*
> *at the light of your arrows as they sped,*
> *at the flash of your glittering spear.*
> ¹² *You marched through the earth in fury;*
> *you threshed the nations in anger.*
> ¹³ *You went out for the salvation of your people,*
> *for the salvation of your anointed.*
> *You crushed the head of the house of the wicked,*
> *laying him bare from thigh to neck. Selah*
> ¹⁴ *You pierced with his own arrows the heads of his warriors,*
> *who came like a whirlwind to scatter me,*
> *rejoicing as if to devour the poor in secret.*
> ¹⁵ *You trampled the sea with your horses,*
> *the surging of mighty waters. (3:3-15; ESV)*

Our hope springs eternal, it is sustained, because **first**, we know God to be the *Holy One*. He is morally pure, totally separate from and repulsed by evil, and cannot allow that evil to go on indefinitely. He will put a stop to it. He will ultimately make things right. You can count on it! God will bring down the ungodly in Israel, the vile Babylonians, and the current adversaries of his people. As Roberts states, holiness is "the radical and dangerous otherness of God, his separation and elevation over all possible rivals."[26] J. I. Packer adds, "The word signifies everything about God that sets him apart from us and makes him an object of awe, adoration, and dread to us."[27] One day our world will be free from, forever separated from, and delivered from every expression or effect of sin. His holiness demands it. Therefore, we can live for it. We can rest assured of it.

Second, we have hope because of the glory of God's *splendor.* Now exactly what does that mean? God's splendor is the dazzling brilliance, the white-hot light, the blazing fire of his presence filling the heavens. As Amerding remarks, it is reminiscent of the "awe-inspiring radiance that characterized his descent on Mount Sinai – a light as brilliant as the lightening that accompanied that event, incandescent with his glory."[28] Just as the heavens were lit up at creation and at Sinai, they will one day be ablaze with the glory of the armies of heaven filling the sky at Christ's return. Yes, there will be the carnage of this final battle to vanquish the forces of evil, but it will be followed by a glorious reign of peace in a brand-new safe world. Accordingly, our hope looks back and springs forward to the day when the light of God's presence will dissipate the darkness of the universe and forever clothe it with the splendor and glow of the new creation. Imagine the Son-rise then!

Third, we have hope because of God's colossal *power* – his ability to do anything, indeed everything, that his holy will desires! So immense is that power, that the display of it must be veiled and its exercise tempered. Negatively, God could, in an instant, vaporize the entire universe, bringing it to extinction. The apostle Peter speaks of a coming day of judgment when *"the heavens will pass away with a roar, and the heavenly bodies will be burnt up and dissolved."* (II Peter 3:10 ESV) Positively,

---

26 Roberts, *Nahum, Habakkuk, Zephaniah*, p.151.

27 J. I. Packer, *Concise Theology.* P. 43.

28 Amerding, p. 526.

Christ mercifully holds all things together preventing Creation from disintegrating into chaos and collapsing into ruin (Colossians 1:17).

As you read these coming verses you may rightly say, "I don't see much hope here." Is not the Divine Warrior on the rampage? What we will see is that Habakkuk's prayer demonstrates God's power over every part of creation. And if he has the power to judge, he also has the power to bless, if the power to inflict disease, then the power to heal disease, if the power to bring to ruin, then the power to rebuild and re-new. When sin has rightly been judged, salvation will finally and fully be realized. His justice and holiness demands it. His love and mercy looks beyond it – from Paradise lost to Paradise regained.

God has power over disease. Indeed, it was plague and pestilence that he used in liberating the Israelites from Egypt (Exodus 7:8-11; 10) and judging his people for worshiping the golden calf at Mount Sinai. Plague and pestilence will also be part of the divine entourage, the rav-ishes of war, the weapons in God's arsenal as he wars against Babylon. But the same power over disease which devastated Egypt and Babylon, is the same power that mends the broken hearted and ultimately heals all our diseases. The lame shall surely walk, the blind shall see, the deaf shall hear, the mute shall speak and the dead shall live again: (Isaiah 61:1; 53:5; 35:5-6; 26:19).

God has power over nature. This passage is filled with vivid poetic im-agery displaying God's power over the mountains, the rivers, the seas, and the sun and moon - both in the past and the future. God has only to stop and give a threatening glance and a violent earthquake ensues, so powerful that it levels the terrain around it. The mountains fall to pieces writhing like a mother in childbirth. The "ancient hills collapse like a spent balloon" (*The Message*). Indeed, the "age-old" mountains have come face to face with their "age-less" Creator.

God had demonstrated this power over the Nile when he turned it to blood and the Red Sea and Jordan when he parted their waves. All this had been done to deliver his people Israel. And the God who piled up the waters of the Red Sea is the same God who brought the raging waves of the worldwide flood (Genesis 7:11; 8:2) and forces the depths of the deep to lift her hands in full surrender. Therefore "as the Babylonian comes to heap judgment on God's people, he may expect an awesome retaliation from the same One who has smitten rivers and seas in the past."[29]

But there is more! God is further seen as sovereign over the celestial bodies. The prophet hearkens back to the longest day in history when the sun and moon stood still (Joshua 10:12-13). The scene is a miracle of cosmic proportions as God rains hailstones from heaven, and causes the earth to cease in its rotation, till he has devastated and demolished Israel's enemies. Even the sun and moon must do his bidding.

God has power over the nations They are seen as shaken – terrified at the prospect of God's imminent punishment. Cushan and Midian (Arab nomadic tribes in the region) tremble, consumed with apprehension, as the Divine Warrior furiously begins his march across the earth. The world has become his "threshing floor." Just as the ancient farmer violently beats his grain so the Lord tramples and crushes evil nations underfoot. Their armaments are no match for the lightning bolts from his hand, the arrows of his bow, the glitter of his spear, his chariot of salvation. Irresistible are his weapons, his agents of war, and so complete his victory, that the enemy (Egypt in the past, Babylon in the near future, the Antichrist at the end of history) is left decapitated (without a leader), humiliated - stripped naked from thigh to neck.

What is all this telling us? The Holy God regaled in splendor, unlimited in power will stop at nothing to save his people. This is faith's hope! The whole purpose of this Psalm is to picture God demolishing the enemies of his people in order to bring about their final and full deliverance. Just as he delivered Israel from Egypt through his anointed one Moses, so he will ultimately deliver all of creation through the Messiah, King Jesus. Just as God marshalled his weapons against Babylon, so will Christ destroy God's enemies at Armageddon. There are clear eschatological and universal overtones here mirroring

---

29 Robertson, p. 231.

the convulsions in nature, the time of intense tribulation, and the unleashing of God's wrath at the end of the present age (cf. Ps. 97:3-5; Isa. 29:6; Joel 3:13-16; Nah. 1:1-8; Zech. 14:1-4; Rev. 16:18-21).

And now comes Habakkuk's response to this close encounter with God (3:16-19). His insides shudder, his lips quiver, his body goes limp, and his legs buckle. All emotional and physical strength has left him. But this is where faith steps in, where faith stands tall. As the dark creeps in around him, the resolve of hope revives him. He can and will wait for the salvation of the Lord.

What is amazing is that He does so anticipating an economic calamity immediately on the horizon. In his agrarian society the loss of the fig, wine, and olive industry, the decimation of the fields, flocks and herds meant not only economic ruin but widespread starvation. This would surely accompany the imminent large-scaled Babylonian invasion.

"But I will sing joyful praise," he announces, "I will rejoice in the Lord my God!" How amazing! How unbelievable! The prophet's joy is a spring of hope flowing from the fountain of his faith. And this is no ordinary joy. This is "turning cartwheels" (*The Message*, 3:18), jumping up and down joy. Why? His heart and mind are so transfixed on God that he is elevated above the tyranny and trouble of the world around him. It is one thing to appreciate and revel in God's goodness when all is "on the up and up." It is quite another to praise God in the midst of adversity. But when God has become the source of your strength, the certainty of things hoped for, the preeminent object of your affections, then a song bursts forth even from within a prison's walls (Acts 16).

Habakkuk exclaims, "Yahweh, my Lord, is my strength!" No stronger words are available in his language to describe the wonder, majesty, and power of God.[30] No greater argument can be raised for his jubilant confidence. His hope is in the God who made promises, who entered into a covenant relationship with Abraham, Isaac, Jacob, David, and yes, even Habakkuk. The God of Israel will not fail him. He can face

---

30 Kenneth Barker and Waylon Bailey, p. 429.

the future. He can skip across the mountain tops with the sure-footed confidence of the deer. He can live above the fray, make his way up and out of the valley of despair. He can feel like the king of the mountain (The Message, 3:19). And you can too!

You see, this song-burst is not for the prophet alone; its musical notation commends this hymn to be sung by the ensuing generations.[31] It is our song as it was theirs. We too can sing as we embark on or as we enlarge our faith journey. In the words of a simple chorus I sang as a child, "Sing, when the day is bright, sing through the darkest night, every day, all the way, let us sing, sing, sing!" We sing because our hope is in the Lord, rooted in who he is and what he has done. We sing, "Holy, holy, holy is the Lord God Almighty; the earth is filled with his glory" (Isaiah 6:3). We sing, "The splendor of the king clothed in majesty, let all the earth rejoice."[32] Our chorus resounds as we sing of "the mighty power of God that made the mountains rise, that spread the flowing seas abroad and built the lofty skies."[33] In the words of the Virgin Mary,

> *My soul magnifies the Lord,*
> [47] *and my spirit rejoices in God my Savior...*
> [51] *He has shown strength with his arm;*
> *he has scattered the proud in the thoughts of their hearts;*
> [52] *he has brought down the mighty from their thrones*
> *and exalted those of humble estate;*
> [53] *he has filled the hungry with good things,*
> *and the rich he has sent away empty.*
> [54] *He has helped his servant Israel,*
> *in remembrance of his mercy,*
> [55] *as he spoke to our fathers,*
> *to Abraham and to his offspring forever. (Luke 1:46-55 ESV)*

---

31 Robertson, Nahum, Habakkuk, Zephaniah, 247-48.

32 From Chris Tomlin's song, *How Great Is Our God.*

33 From Isaac Watts' hymn, *I Sing the Mighty Power of God.*

When faith is all you've got left, faith is enough! Why? Because the faith we speak of is not simply a possibility, it is an absolute surety. It is not wishful thinking, it is a settled confidence in God's promises (Hebrews 11:1). Faith's hope is anchored in the indubitable, undeniable future God has promised us through the person and work of Christ. As J. Wilber Chapman's timeless hymn exclaims:

> *One day the trumpet will sound for His coming,*
> *One day the skies with His glories will shine;*
> *Wonderful day, my beloved ones bringing;*
> *Glorious Savior, this Jesus is mine!*

CHAPTER 6

Putting It All Together!

§

What I have discovered is that when faith is "all you've got left," faith is more than enough. Of course, it is imperative that you have some sense of "what faith" I am talking about. And how can faith be "more than enough" when I am backed into a corner with seemingly no way out. Like many of you, I have experienced financial woes, relational failures, sudden tragedies, debilitating chronic illnesses, life goal disappointments, haunting memories, and daily spiritual battles. What could possibly ground me in the throes of all these? What faith has driven me through and propelled me to live above, not "under the circumstances?"

Let me begin by saying that this faith is an implicit active trust, a certain conviction based on evidence – mountains of corroborating evidence. It involves my whole person and is as much cerebral, a willful act of the mind, as it is a passion of the heart. It is a moment by moment trust and conviction that collectively permeate my thoughts, my words, my acts, my plans, my demeanor. It is a way of life!

But above all it is a relationship. I am just one in a host of others who have become a part of a family whose genealogy goes back to the very beginning of history – the days of Abel, Enoch and Abraham. I am a son of God, a devoted follower of Christ. I have been blessed to enter into a daily, yet eternal, relationship with God through Christ's gracious unmerited work on my behalf. He lived, for me, the perfect life God required in order that I might enter heaven. He took the full punishment for my countless sins that God's holiness and justice demanded. There would be no faith, and no reason to exercise faith, apart from being in relationship with the one who is "the founder and perfecter of our faith" (Hebrews 12:2). It has been my highest joy to trust in all that Jesus has done, and is doing and will do, as my Savior and my Master.

As we have seen, this life of faith allows me, indeed it encourages me, to ask the hard questions. I am not an automaton robotically checking all the right boxes devoid of emotion. God asks me to come seeking, asking, pounding on the doors of heaven sharing every feeling that churns inside me when caught up in the agony of life's incongruities, inequities, and injustices. There is no such thing as off limits or out of bounds in these conversations with him. *There is a release, a freedom that is gained as I dump my burdens in His lap. I can whisper, sob, even yell if I must. I come with my questions. As I tarry, I leave with His peace.* And I am reminded that many have shared the same, indeed far worse, life experiences and emotions throughout the ages and even now. See Psalm 5, 10, 17, 35, 58, 59, 69, 70, 77, 79, 83, 109, 129, 137, and 140, for example. **Authentic faith, a faith that goes the distance, is an *honest* faith!**

I can ask faith's questions knowing that many are already answered in Scripture. The Bible tells me who created me, why he created me, in general what I am to do here, the over-all reasons for suffering, where history is headed, and where I am going when I leave this life. For example, I am given enormous value and worth knowing I am made in God's image (male and female, Genesis 1:26-27) with a complex intellect, creativity, sense of morality, emotions and the free will to choose.

I have the firm conviction that God is not caught off guard with anything that I might ask and that he will answer with a "Yes! No! or Wait! *When God does not explain now, I know he will explain later. And I am assured that either the answer is beyond my comprehension or beyond my ability to bear at the moment.* Some things are better left unsaid, unanswered. As Charles Spurgeon once said, "When we cannot trace his hand, we must trust his heart."

Authentic faith, a faith that goes the distance, is a *humble* faith. By humble we mean the inner strength and outward deference that comes from an accurate view of one's self, and the desire to reflect the mindset modeled by the life and death of our Lord and Savior Jesus Christ (Philippians 2:1-5). We realize that we are fully dependent upon God, that nothing we have or are is ultimately the work of our own creation, but the gifts of God's love and grace. Accordingly, we are eager to serve others, to defer or submit to their needs even at the setting aside of our own. There is no depth too low to stoop to if it means their stepping up into the family and the future of the people of God. Humility is meekness but definitely not weakness. It is wholly "other-centeredness" not obsessive self-deprecation. It takes far more emotional strength and character to be a Mother Teresa than a Vladimir Putin.

What I have come to realize is that a humble attitude is not only the way out of the valley of despair, it is the certain path to navigating the minefields - the sure hope to ending well. Why!

1. *A humble attitude has an accurate healthy view of the dangers and demise of evil.*

It does not take it for granted. It realizes that you cannot handle destructive habits and sinful practices, the lure of dubious relationships, and the fiery darts of your enemies entirely on your own. Absent the supernatural unlimited power of God, evil will take you down. But it is equally assured that victory is certain through the enablement of God working in you and through others. For the humble, victory, however small, is always imminent! Why? They take the battle, and the enemy, seriously and so avoid the pitfalls along the way. Day by day they see "small wins" that point to a climatic victory in the future. A humble mind keeps them ever on the alert and yet confident that together, with God's help, they will see the cancer evil, step by step dismantled, till it reaches its deserved end.

2. *A humble attitude has an accurate view of the purpose and promise of suffering.*

We cannot avoid suffering. It will enter every facet of our lives. Therefore, to be consumed with constant anger or to be decimated by ongoing depression is not a choice that we wish to make. It simply can't and won't help. It won't help to endlessly declare, "I don't deserve this!" Whether you do, or do not, will not make things better. But what will, is to see suffering more as a scalpel than a sword.

Further, we "will seldom know the micro reasons for our sufferings, but the Bible does give us faith-sustaining macro reasons."[34] What then is the purpose and promise of suffering? Here are three of them. *First, suffering is God's tool to lead us to repentance (a turning away from destructive beliefs and behaviors in humble confession) that leads to healing, restoration, obedience and maturity.* Much of our suffering is self-afflicted. We eat wrongly, speak wrongly, think wrongly, work wrongly…and then we bear the rotted fruit of our actions. But when we agree with God about the repugnance of these thoughts and actions, we receive not only full forgiveness, restored intimacy, but we are empowered to live in an obedient, prudent life-giving way that frees us from further heartaches in the future. Why? We gradually replace the destructive behaviors of anger, malice, slander, lust, obscenities, profanities with the productive behaviors of humility, patience, honesty, self-control, purity and encouragement (Hebrews 12:6-11; James 1:2-4; Galatians 5:19-23). Life's trials crush our trouble-breeding pride and replace it with a humbled mind. And with this new outlook comes new outcomes.

Second, suffering is God's tool to force you to rely on him which will lead not only to a life of victory here, but a glimpse, a preview of an eternity of unsurpassed indescribable joy there (Second Corinthians 1:8-9; 4:17). When God has removed all of your props, all that gives you the smugness of self-sufficiency, he is now able to display his unlimited power unhindered through you and in you. All our fretting over (and even the

---

34 See http://www.desiringgod.org/articles/five-purposes-for-suffering

agonies of) momentary sufferings when compared to an eternity without them (multiplied trillions of years and beyond) seem small, even foolish. When we look away from our problems and fix our eyes on what is coming, the new heaven and earth, we are lost in the wonder of exploring the galaxies, picnicking in the Edenic gardens, invigorating conversations with the saints of all the ages, being held in the arms of our Creator and Savior. O what a day that will be!

Third, suffering is God's tool to allow us the privilege of sharing in the sufferings of Christ with the promise of getting to know him even better (Philippians 3:10). We can never really know all that Christ went through, all that he suffered, when he laid aside the trappings of glory to travel the trail of tears for us. But when we are misunderstood, we are reminded that he was misunderstood. When we are maligned, when we are misquoted, when we are marginalized, when we are ostracized, when we are persecuted, we begin to understand the depths to which he plunged to deliver us from sin, separation and Satan. And if we are called to give our lives for him, we will be given an even better glimpse of the enormity of the task, the infinitude of a love that would stop at nothing less than the ultimate sacrifice to give us the ultimate best, an eternity with him. Is it not worth all our pains and sorrows to share, however small it is, in his?

Authentic faith, a faith that goes the distance, is a *persevering* faith. By perseverance we mean "staying power (Ropes), active steadfastness (Laws)." (See James 1:3, Romans 5:4) This is not some "passive submission to circumstances, but a strong, active, challenging response."[35] This is a faith that doesn't give up, doesn't give in, but plows through, faces head on the trial in front of him or her. I have personally been called to such perseverance through a number of physical maladies including a bout with cancer, acute and chronic pancreatitis, complicated hereditary spastic paraplegia and more. Yet what I have faced is pitifully small when compared to the enormous afflictions suffered by the Apostle Paul (See Second Corinthians 11:16-29)

---

35 Douglas Moo, *The Letter of James*, p. 60.

or countless saints today in parts of the Middle East, Africa, and Asia. Where did they get that remarkable faith? How does faith persevere?

First, you realize that as faith perseveres through suffering, it authenti-cates, gives evidence, that you are God's child (Second Thessalonians 1:4-5; First Peter 1:7). Paul has told us that many difficulties and persecutions follow those who believe in Christ (Acts 14:22). Jesus said that if they persecuted him they would persecute all who follow him (John 15:20). When you are willing and enabled to endure suffering, you demon-strate both the reality and the maturity of your faith. Only those who have shared in Christ's sufferings will share in his glory when he comes again (Romans 8:17). I can therefore be comforted with the assurance that I am indeed Christ's own.

Second, you persist because you are assured that the injustice that you have endured at the hands of your persecutors will be vindicated (Second Thessalonians 1: 6-10). We will say more about this later.

Third, you persevere, remain steadfast, because your trials lead to the crown jewel of being perfect and complete, lacking nothing, in Christ (James 1:2-4). We press forward, staying at it, even as trials of every kind (physical, emotional, relational, etc.) assault us from every direction (at home, at work, domestic and foreign). Why? They refine us, gradually removing all the impurities and imperfections from our lives. They drive us to a complete dependence on God's wisdom and power and free us from the alarming consequences and ruin of self-reliance and self -centered-ness. We come to understand trials as the path to a well-rounded, fully developed Christian character in the near future and a foretaste of our absolute perfection in eternity. There is an "already, not yet" aspect to what James is saying.

Paul excites us further with the reality that not only does our per-severance lead to a step by step, fully developed Christian character, it also produces an unquenchable hope (Romans 5:3-5). This hope will not embarrass or shame us when we stand before God someday. Why? The love from God that entered our heart through the Holy Spirit when we received Christ as our Savior is an ever-present testimony that we can never be separated from his love now or in the future (See Romans 8:3-39). His love never changes!

Authentic faith, a faith that goes the distance, will be an avenged faith. The enemies of God will not have the final word. God will avenge the righteous. The virulent attacks and seething acrimony of the God haters will cease and desist. As Paul writes, *"Since indeed God considers it just to repay with affliction those who afflict you, ⁷ and to grant relief to you who are afflicted… when the Lord Jesus is revealed from heaven with his mighty angels ⁸ in flaming fire, inflicting vengeance on those who do not know God and on those who do not obey the gospel of our Lord Jesus. ⁹ They will suffer the punishment of eternal destruction, away from the presence of the Lord and from the glory of his might, ¹⁰ when he comes on that day to be glorified in his saints, and to be marveled at among all who have believed"* (Second Thessalonians 1:6-10 ESV) John Stott writes, "We see the malice, cruelty, power and arrogance of the evil men who persecute. We see also the sufferings of the people of God, who are opposed, ridiculed, boycotted, harassed, imprisoned, tortured and killed. In other words, what we see is injustice the wicked flourishing and the righteous suffering. It seems completely topsy-turvy." [35] But, perhaps that day will soon come to an end!

The people of God rest assured with the comfort that all will one day be made right. Those who have brutalized Christ's followers, whether in word or deed, will receive their just reward. It is not ours to avenge. Vengeance belongs to God. Those who love God and others are thankfully not consumed by the hate of revenge, but are placated and assuaged by the hope of the resplendent triumphant glory that is coming. I am reminded of the song our college chorale reveled in over forty years ago. How often it returns to resound within my heart and head:

> When He shall come, resplendent in His glory,
> To take His own from out this vale of night,

---

35 John Stott, *The Bible Speaks Today: The Message of 1&2 Thessalonians*, p. 147.

O may I know the joy at His appearing
Only at morn to walk with Him in white!

When I shall stand within the court of Heaven
Where white-robed pilgrims pass before my sight
Earth's martyred saints and blood-washed overcomers
These then are they who walk with Him in white!

When He shall call, from earth's remotest corners,
All who have stood triumphant in His might,
O to be worthy then to stand beside them,
And in that morn to walk with Him in white! [36]

Finally, ***Authentic faith, a faith that goes the distance, is a hope-driven faith.*** As we have discovered this is not a "hope so' groundless faith. It is a confident assurance, a certain expectation, an active, ongoing, committed trust that is the underpinning of a Christian's way of life (Hebrews 11:1; 6:18-20). This, our hope, is grounded in the person and work of our God and Savior, Jesus Christ (First Timothy 1:1).

As we look back we are made confident by the sovereign fulfillment of God's promises in the salvation plan of God in history past:

1) Right after man sinned and was driven from the Garden of Eden, God promised that he would crush the serpent's (Satan's) head through one of the descendants of Eve (Genesis 3:15). He did! How? The devil was dealt a mortal wound through the cross. Christ broke Satan's paralyzing fear of eternal death by receiving the capital punishment due for our sins (Hebrews 2:14-15).

2) God promised that a virgin would miraculously conceive a son through the Holy Spirit who would be called Immanuel,

---

36 *When He Shall Come*, Words and Music by Almeda Pearce, Arranged by Camp Kirkland.

meaning "God is with us!" (Isaiah 7:14; Luke 1:34-35). Seven hundred years later, she did (Matthew 1:23). Why does that matter? Our hope is grounded in the fact that Jesus lived the sinless life for us we could not live. His being a child of Mary assured his true humanity. His conception by the Holy Spirit assured his freedom from inherited or original sin. His being God was also necessary. Why? Because salvation can only come from the LORD (Psalm 3:8; Jonah 2:9).

3) God spoke through the prophets predicting where the Messiah would be born (in an insignificant town, Bethlehem, Micah 5:2), how he would he would suffer and die for our sins (Isaiah 53; Psalm 22:12-16), and that the grave could not hold him captive for he would rise again! (Psalm 16:10). All these prophesies were fulfilled. All these promises were kept! (Matthew 2:1, First Corinthians 15:1-11). If these were, will not ours?

As we look to the present we see almost daily Jesus's promises fulfilled to provide "another Comforter" the Holy Spirit (John 14:16) who would guide us (Romans 8:14) and illuminate the truth to us (John 14:17; 16:13) serving as the divine resident teacher within our hearts. We hear him whisper assuring words that we are truly a child of God (Romans 8:16). We remember the day when, as Jesus promised, the Spirit convicted and convinced us of the ugliness of our sin, our need for Christ's perfect righteousness, and God's judgment both of Satan and of us if we spurned the Gospel message (John 16:8-10; John 3:17). We see the wonder of the promised Spirit's empowerment to be a witness for Christ (Acts 1:8), the Spirit's enablement when we do not know how to pray (Romans 8: 26), and the "sword of the Spirit" as our weapon against the schemes of the Devil (Ephesians 6: 17). But perhaps the most telling is the ongoing amazing transformation of the Spirit as he liberates us from sinful practices and causes us to become more clearly reflections of the character of God (Second Corinthians 3:18; Galatians 5:19-24). Indeed, the sense that we don't really fit in or belong to the world's system, that we are strangers and exiles (Hebrews 11:13) meant for another world, is a daily reminder of the hope of Christ's promise of a heavenly home (John 14:3).

If then we can look into the past, reflect on the present, and see the trustworthiness and fulfillment of God's promises, is it not abundantly clear that **we can trust God's promises for the future**. Our faith is not a blind faith, but is almost daily proven to be as certain as the air we breathe. So, when we are told that we will rise again (First Thessalonians 4:13-17; First Corinthians 15:51-58), will we not rise? When we are told that we will live forever in a new heaven and new earth (Revelation 21 and 22), can we not respond with joy? We most assuredly can! This is what brings us through the dark night of the soul. This is what causes us to press on when others cry that there is no way out, that there is no hope left. Our hope cannot be extinguished. It is not a fuzzy feeling, a wisp of the imagination, a delusion of the mind. It is a person who anchors us in the storms of life. In the words of Chris Tomlin:

> There's a peace I've come to know
> Though my heart and flesh may fail
> There's an anchor for my soul
> I can say, It is well.
>
> Jesus has overcome
> and the grave is overwhelmed
> The victory is won
> He is risen from the dead.
>
> And I will rise
> When He calls my name
> No more sorrow, no more pain
> I will rise, on eagle's wings
> Before my God

fall on my knees,
and rise...
I will rise. [37]

We have come to the sum of the matter. I have found, as you may find, that the faith God has placed within me has been more than enough to handle the raging storms of life. Years ago, while watching a movie, "The Hiding Place," Nazi death camp survivor, Corrie ten Boom, forever burned this truth into the fabric of my being, "No pit is so deep that He is not deeper still; with Jesus, even in our darkest moments, the best remains and the very best is yet to be."

---

37 Chris Tomlin, *I will Rise*, 2008 Sixsteprecords

Part Two
Faith's Path

§

Kimberly Allston

PART TWO
FAITH'S PATH

Habakkuk Devotion Outline

WEEK FOUR: HOPE

Day 1: God's History

§

READ GENESIS 1:1 "IN THE beginning, _____...."

God has always existed. He is history, present and future. We have been created for His pleasure.

To know God's history is to know His character. He has always and will always love His people. He created us to love Him and be loved by Him. His history is His people - you and me. He lovingly pursues His people to be in relationship with Him. When our hearts receive his son, Jesus, we immediately begin a new beginning, a new history.

Our history and God's history become one. We are forever intertwined with Him.

Let's look at God's history through His people.

First was Adam and Eve. From their line of descendants, came Noah. From Noah's descendants came Abraham.

Abraham had a son, Isaac, and then a grandson, Jacob. Jacob then had 12 sons: Reuben, Simeon, Levi, Judah, Issachar, Zebulun, Gad, Asher, Joseph, Benjamin, Dan, Naphtali.

God changed Jacob's name to Israel and eventually his sons would be known as the 12 tribes of Israel (using Israel as the new name of Jacob and the name of the land that would follow). God's people were now known as Israelites.

Side Note: Joseph's sons, Ephraim and Manasseh, are blessed by Jacob and become their own tribes instead of a tribe of Joseph.

Also, a different tribe is left out in different locations of the Old Testament.

So let's recap our history timeline. Fill in the blanks by order of descendants.

Adam, _____, Abraham, _____, Jacob who was later re-named _____.

Jacob's 12 sons:
Reuben, _____, _____, Levi, _____,
Issachar, _____, Gad, _____, _____,
Benjamin, Dan, _____.

Who were the 2 sons of Joseph that were blessed by his father, Jacob, and would eventually have their own tribes?
_____, _____

All of Jacob's 12 sons eventually moved to Egypt where the Israelites multiplied and the tribes became great in number. Because of their great numbers, the Egyptian Pharaoh made the Israelites slaves so they could not overthrow his power.

From the descendants of the tribe of Levi came Moses.
From the descendants of the tribe of Ephraim came Joshua.

God would use Moses to lead the Israelites out of slavery in Egypt. Then God would use Joshua to lead the Israelites into the land of Canaan which God had promised to them.

Read Exodus 3:7-8. The land of Canaan is described as a land flowing with _____ and _____.

The Israelites also named Canaan the Promised Land because God had promised them this land to dwell in.

While the Israelites traveled from Egypt to Canaan (which took 40 years), God repeatedly gave them very clear instructions. These instructions would become known as the 10 commandments.

Look at Deuteronomy 5:6-7. What is God's #1 commandment:

_____

(verse 7)

God is a God of clarity. He told (and warned) the Israelites many, many times that He had to be first in their lives.

Read Deuteronomy chapter 6.

1. Why is it important for the Israelites (and us today) to always obey God? (Verse 24)

_____

2. Who were the Israelites instructed to tell about God's commandments? _____

Why?_____

(verses 20-21)

Read Deuteronomy 30:15-20.

God gives His people the choice of either _____ or _____ (verse 19).

If the Israelites obey, how does God say He will bless them (verse 16)?

_____

If the Israelites disobey, how does God say He will curse them (verses 17 and 18)?

_____

God's history has always been through His people and His promises. In this devotional series, we will learn how God is faithful to His word - through good times and hard times. His story is our story. His history is our history.

Day 2: Israel's History

§

BEFORE WE CAN KNOW HABAKKUK'S history, we first have to know the history of his people.

God's people, the Israelites, have quite a varied history. From their sin of disobedience, their history is full of hard times and heartache. They continually ignored God's warnings for their actions. Because of these sins, Habakkuk would have to inform the people of God's judgment for their sins.

In yesterday's devotion, we learned that Moses led the Israelites out of slavery from Egypt. After 40 years of wandering in the desert, the Israelites finally are at their destination of the promised land, Canaan.

Joshua, the new leader of the Israelites, leads the people into Canaan to take possession of the land that God had promised them.

God's instructions were for the Israelites to completely drive out the current people in the land of Canaan - the Canaanites. The Israelites drove out most of them but not all. This would later cause many problems for the Israelites.

Joshua divided the land into 12 areas with each area of land given to the 12 tribes of Israel. These 12 tribes come from Jacob who had 12 sons. Each son (and 2 grandsons) became a tribe of people that were then known by their given name. However, Levi, the priestly tribe, had no land allotment, and Joseph's allotment went to his two sons.

The land of Canaan, which becomes known as the land of Israel, is one nation.. It is first ruled by elders, then judges, then kings. During the rule of King Saul (Israel's first king), Israel is one nation. After King Saul dies, David becomes king. Israel is united during David's reign except for the first 7 1/2 years of his rule.

David, a descendant from the tribe of Judah, is given a promise by God that his family line will not be destroyed. From this family line (the tribe of Judah), our Savior, Jesus Christ, descended.

After King David, his son Solomon becomes king. Israel is united during Solomon's reign. Because of the sins by King Solomon, God says the consequences will be that the land of Israel will be divided into 2 nations with many tensions and battles between those 2 nations. The division will occur during the rule of Solomon's son, Rehoboam.

Read 1 Kings 11:9-13
"The Lord became angry with _____ because his heart had turned away from the Lord, the God of Israel, who had appeared to him twice. Although he had forbidden Solomon to follow other _____, Solomon did not keep the Lord's command. So the Lord said to Solomon, "'Since this is your attitude and you have not kept my _____ and my decrees, which I have commanded you, I will most certainly tear the kingdom away from you and give it to one of your _____. Nevertheless, for the sake of David

your father, I will not do it during your lifetime. I will tear it out of the hand of your _____. Yet I will not tear the whole kingdom from him, but will give him one tribe for the sake of _____ my servant and for the sake of _____, which I have chosen.'"

The division resulted into the kingdom being divided into the Northern Kingdom (Israel) and Southern Kingdom (Judah). The Southern Kingdom is called Judah and consists of 2 of the tribes (Judah and Benjamin). The Northern Kingdom is called Israel and consists of the remaining 10 tribes.

The nation will be divided for several hundred years. During this time, each kingdom will have their own king.

In our study, we will focus primarily on the Southern Kingdom. This kingdom will have a mix of good and evil kings. Let's learn about them.

Here is the line of kings for the Southern Kingdom:

Rehoboah
2 Chronicles 12:14 - Rehoboah did _____ in the eyes of the Lord because _____.

Abijah
I Kings 15:3 - Abijah committed all the _____ his father had done before him; his _____ was not fully devoted to the Lord his God, as the heart of David his forefather had been.

Asa
I Kings 15:11 - Asa did what was _____ in the eyes of the Lord.

Jehoshaphat
I Kings 22:43 - In everything he walked in the ways of his father, _____, and did not stray from them; he did what was _____ in the eyes of the Lord.

Jehoram
2 Kings 8:18-19 - He did _____ in the eyes of the Lord. Nevertheless, for the sake of His servant David, the Lord was not willing to destroy _____. He had promised to maintain a lamp for David and his _____.

Ahaziah
2 Chronicles 22:4 - He did _____ in the eyes of the Lord.

Joash
2 Kings 11:21 - Joash was _____ years old when he began to reign.
2 Kings 12:2 - Joash did what was _____ in the eyes of the Lord all the years Jehoiada the priest instructed him.

Amaziah
2 Chronicles 25:2 - Amaziah did what was _____ in the eyes of the Lord, but not _____.

Azariah (also called Uzziah)
2 Chronicles 26:4-5 - He did what was _____ in the eyes of the Lord, just as his father _____ had done. He sought God during the days of Zechariah (God's prophet), who instructed him in the fear of God. As long as he sought the Lord, God gave him _____.

Jotham
2 Chronicles 27:2 - He did what was _____ in the eyes of the Lord.

Ahaz
2 Chronicles 28:1 - He did or did not (circle one) do what was right in the eyes of the Lord.

Hezekiah
2 Chronicles 29:2 - He did what was _____ in the eyes of the Lord..

Manasseh
2 Chronicles 33:2 - He did _____ in the eyes of the Lord.

Amon
2 Chronicles 33:22 - He did _____ in the eyes of the Lord.

Josiah
2 Chronicles 34:2 - He did what was _____ in the eyes of the Lord and walked in the ways of his (fore)father David, not turning aside to the _____ or to the _____.

After Josiah's death, his first son, Jehoahaz, is king for three months. Then Josiah's other son, Eliakim (later renamed Jehoiakim) ruled for 11 years. Then Jehoiakim's son, Jehoiachin became king for 3 months. After this, his uncle, Zedekiah, reigned for 11 years.

Side Note: Josiah was Judah's last strong and good king. After his death, the Southern Kingdom (Judah) began to weaken and would soon be overtaken and controlled by the Babylonians and its king, Nebuchadnezzar. Nebuchadnezzar would allow Josiah's descendants to rule over Judah's capital, Jerusalem, but he still maintained control and even invaded Judah and took many of its people into captivity for 70 years.

Count how many kings were evil in Israel's history and write the number here _____.

There were a lot more evil kings than good kings. It's important to realize that the Israelites followed the ways of their king. If a king did not worship God, the majority of the people didn't either. If the king did worship God, the people did as well. The kings had a tremendous influence on whom the people worshiped. With so many evil kings, Israel continued to go against God despite His constant warnings.

The Babylonian invasion and captivity will be the focus of Habakkuk's prophecy to God's people. This event will shape Habakkuk's life and his relationship with God.

The captivity of Judah's people for 70 years is all part of God's plan. But why such a harsh plan? Habakkuk will ask God this same question.

God shares his answer with us in His word. Look at 2 Chronicles 36:14-21:
Furthermore, all the leaders of the priests and the people became more and more unfaithful, following all the detestable practices of the nations and defiling the temple of the Lord, which He had consecrated in Jerusalem. The Lord, the God of their fathers, sent word to them through His messengers again and again, because He had pity on His people and on His dwelling place. But they mocked God's messengers, despised His words and scoffed at His prophets until the wrath of the Lord was aroused against His people and there was no remedy. He brought up against them the king of the Babylonians, who killed their young men with the sword in the sanctuary, and spared neither young man nor young woman, old man or aged. God handed all of them over to Nebuchadnezzar. He carried to Babylon all the articles from the temple of God, both large and small, and the treasures of the Lord's temple and the treasures of the king and his officials. They set fire to God's temple and broke down the wall of Jerusalem; they burned all the palaces and destroyed everything of value there. He carried into exile to Babylon the remnant, who escaped from the sword, and they

became servants to him and his sons until the kingdom of Persia came to power. The land enjoyed its sabbath rests; all the time of its desolation it rested, until the seventy years were completed in fulfillment of the word of the Lord spoken by Jeremiah.

The Lord gives us 2 reasons for Judah's captivity:

1. Constant idolatry and worship of other gods. We see this consistently with evil kings ruling Judah.

Remember God's first commandment from Week 1, Day 1?
You shall not have any _____ before _____.

2. Failure to observe the sabbatical years of rest (referenced in God's instructions to the Israelites in Leviticus 25:2-7)

This is God's fourth command. Look at Deuteronomy 5:12-13 - Observe the _____ day by keeping it _____, as the Lord God has commanded you. _____ days you shall labor and do all your work, but the _____ day is a Sabbath to the Lord your God. On it you shall not do any work.

It is interesting to note that the Israelites observed the sabbath during their 70 years of captivity.

Because the Israelites broke these commands over and over and over again, He allowed the Babylonians to invade and capture. We will learn in the days ahead how God converses with Habakkuk about this decision and ultimately brings triumph out of tragedy.

Day 3: Habakkuk's History

§

HABAKKUK'S NAME MEANS EMBRACER. IT is a unique name. I've never met a person named Habakkuk. There isn't another person in the Bible with this name.

Let's look at the definition of embracer. Embracer means a) holding close with the arms - usually as an expression of affection; b) eager acceptance.

Habakkuk had the perfect name because he embraced God even in the difficult times. He embraced God instead of his circumstances. Habakkuk is a great example for us on completely embracing God and His will (even when it isn't our will).

How do you embrace God during difficult times?

A) from a distance
B) up close but with reservations
C) completely - no matter the circumstances

If you circled A or B, what do you think prevents you from embracing God completely?

_____

Habakkuk was a prophet. A prophet's job was to inform God's people of God's messages. The prophet had to share the message whether it was good news for the people or bad news.

Habakkuk was commissioned with the task of informing God's people of the upcoming invasion and captivity that they would endure. This was not good news for the Israelites and certainly not well received. Prophets had the hard job of accepting the backlash from the people for the unpopular news.

Habakkuk first served as a prophet under King Josiah. Look back on day 2. Was Josiah a good or evil king? _____

Under King Josiah, Habakkuk lived during a time of sincere worship of God and a time that God was #1 in the lives of His people.

After Josiah's death, the kingdom came under the leadership of Jehoiakim. He changes the focus of the kingdom and does evil in the eyes of the Lord. Habakkuk is very frustrated by Jehoiakim's actions. Habakkuk wants the Israelites to worship the one true God. He longs for God's people to repent of their evil ways and return their hearts to God.

The embracer will have his name put to the test. How will Habakkuk embrace God when he learns God's plans of punishment for the Israelite people?

Day 4: Your History

§

WHAT IS YOUR HISTORY WITH God?

Allow me to share some of my history:

As a child growing up, I had many spiritual challenges. I gave my life to Christ and was baptized at age 8. With my father being a pastor, I grew up as a preacher's kid (PK). Some PKs have great experiences in the church. I was not one of those. I saw a side of church people that wasn't pleasant - to say the least. As a child, it's hard to comprehend all the ugliness, discontent, and betrayal that lives inside of the church. I began to hate the church. I couldn't wait to turn 18 so I could go to college and not have to go to church. I completely embraced worldly freedom. It would take many years for me to realize that true freedom is only found with a surrendered life to Christ.

For 18 years, I lived away from God. I only called on God when I needed something or was in trouble. I made many mistakes and lived selfishly for myself. I call this time my convenient Christian years. I only embraced Christ when it was convenient for me.

Soon after my husband and I had our 2nd child, we started to go to church (after much prompting from both our parents). Very slowly, I began to start anew with God. One day I was reading about the Israelites leaving Egypt in Exodus 14:14-15, "The Lord will fight for you; you need only to be still. Then the Lord said to Moses, 'Why are you crying out to me? Tell the Israelites to move on.'" The words "move on" jumped off the page. I clearly heard God say through this verse: ENOUGH! It was time for me to move on from my past hurts with the church.

The only way that I could move on was to completely give my history of hurts over to the Lord. Only through Him would my history be healed.

I then participated in the Beth Moore bible study of Esther. This bible study was a huge turning point for me. I realized how to transform from a convenient Christian to a committed Christian, not just calling on God when I needed something but calling on Him for everything - in all circumstances. Oh how the Lord did a work in me.

Oh how the Lord wants to do a work in you.

Looking back, I realize that God never let me go. He kept working in my life and calling me back to a full life with Him. If you have been away from God, He has never let you go. He is calling you back. He wants to have every part of your history. Give it to Him!

In order to give God our history, we have to be completely truthful with Him and ourselves. God already knows our hearts but He DELIGHTS in our truthful dialogue with Him.

What part of your history needs to be discussed with God in a truthful dialogue? Tell Him then turn it over to Him.

_____

_____

_____

_____

_____

Our history of hurt does not bind us or define us. Our history is part of our story but it's not the entire story. God can use it all for good.

I have had many grieving sessions over the time that I was away from God. I mourn those years. How I wish I had lived differently. BUT God will always use our history of hurt for GOOD. If it wasn't for my 18 years away from God, I don't think I'd be such a committed Christian now. I live to be radical for Him. I want my kids to know that living radically for Christ is the normal, not the exception.

Only in complete surrender to Christ will we ever find real commitment and true freedom.

Are you ready to let God use your history of hurt for good? Why or why not?

_____

_____

_____

Day 5: Read and Receive

§

FOR TODAY, READ CHAPTER 1 in Stan's section. Make notes of the truths that God wants you to receive from this writing.

_____

_____

_____

_____

_____

_____

_____

_____

_____

_____

_____

_____

_____

Day 1: Habakkuk's Honesty to God (Part One)

§

HABAKKUK WAS A GODLY PROPHET who was commissioned by God to inform the Israelites of upcoming hardships.

Habakkuk first lived as a prophet under the reign of King Josiah. Josiah was a _____ king in the eyes of the Lord (look back to week one day 2 if you don't remember).

The time during Josiah's reign was filled with purging the land of idols and worshiping the one true God. The land and its people (including Habakkuk) enjoyed peace and fulfillment. After Josiah's death, his sons did evil in the eyes of the Lord. False idols and wickedness took over the land and prevailed. It is during this time that Habakkuk cries out to the Lord about all the evilness in the land.

Read Habakkuk 1:2-4

Can you feel Habakkuk's frustration? His discouragement? His desperation?

What are Habakkuk's first two words to God in verse 2? _____

Underline those words in your Bible and/or this devotion.

Habakkuk is tired spiritually, emotionally, and physically of all the current ways of God's people. He thinks that God is not listening to Him. We can conclude that this isn't the first time Habakkuk has cried out to God.

Can you relate to Habakkuk? Was there a time that you didn't think God was listening? Maybe you feel that way now. God is ALWAYS listening. He may not answer as fast as we would like. It is our job to keep praying and asking. It is God's job to answer in His perfect timing.

What are the six things that Habakkuk is frustrated about in these verses?

_____,_____,_____,
_____,_____,_____

Do those things remind you of our current condition in the world? This could be our same cry to God today.

In these verses, we learn that Habakkuk wants answers from God on how long and why. How often have we asked God the same things - how long and why?

What is happening in your life now that you are asking God how long and why?

_____
_____

The beauty in these passages is Habakkuk's honesty with God. He lays it all at God's throne. Habakkuk does not hold anything back. Even though he is frustrated, he still shows humility and respect to God.

77

Since God is the creator of emotions, he doesn't want us to hide them from Him.

Are you angry? Are you desperate? Are you sad? Are you mad? Are you disappointed? Are you hurt? Talk to God. Are you being truly honest with God? Even though He already knows, He wants to hear it from you.

With a humble and honest spirit - what do you want to tell God?

_____

_____

What do you want to ask God?

_____

_____

God, I don't understand....

_____

_____

We will soon learn about God's answers to Habakkuk's questions. God has answers for you too.

Day 2: Read and Receive

§

For today, read Chapter 2 in Stan's section. Make notes of the truths that God wants you to receive from this writing.

_____
_____
_____
_____
_____
_____
_____
_____
_____
_____
_____
_____
_____
_____

Day 3: God's Honesty to Habakkuk

§

READ HABAKKUK 1:5-11

In these passages, God is no longer silent to Habakkuk's questions. God completely reveals His plans to the prophet. It is certainly not the answers that Habakkuk expects nor wants to hear. It is even answers that cause Habakkuk to have more questions.

God tells Habakkuk that He is raising up the very evil Babylonians to overtake His people, the Israelites.

God gives a full, detailed description just how evil the Babylonians are. How does God describe them:

_____, _____,
_____, _____,
_____, _____

There is nothing pleasant about the Babylonians. God describes them as a mighty people with no authority. They scoff at rulers and laugh at walled cities. They are completely ruthless. It seems that the situation is hopeless.

Are you facing a situation that seems hopeless?

_____

_____

God wants Habakkuk (and you) to know that He is mightier than anyone or anything. The Babylonians are mighty BUT they are no where near as mighty as God.

Just like God used the Babylonians to bring change to the Israelites, He has all the authority to use whatever means possible to bring change to our lives. A wise woman once told me that God loves us too much to let us continue in sin. He wasn't going to let the Israelites continue in sin and He won't let you either.

Remember that God can only be truthful and honest to us when He answers our questions. As with Habakkuk, it may not be what we expect or want to hear, but it is always for our good.

What honest answers is God giving you? Are you surprised by His answers?

_____

_____

God is still in control. God is mightier than the situation that you are in.

Day 4: Habakkuk's Honesty to God (Part Two)

§

READ HABAKKUK 1:12-13

Well, Habakkuk certainly is perplexed with God's answers. Habakkuk now has more questions than before! Why would God use evil people to punish the Israelites? Why won't God protect His chosen people?

What has the Lord appointed the Babylonians to do in verse 12?

_____

What can God not tolerate in verse 13?

_____

What are the 2 questions that Habakkuk asks God in the latter part of verse 13?

_____

_____

Why? Why? Why?
We often think that we deserve to always know God's reasons. We expect Him to give us immediate answers. We must realize that God does

not have to give us any answers. Many times He doesn't give us all the answers or details for our own protection. God doesn't tell us things that we want to hear; He tells us things that we need to hear. He is always truthful; He never distorts the truth; He never has a hidden agenda.

In Warren W. Wiersbe's book, "Be Amazed," he tells us that "God gives Habakkuk a revelation, not an explanation. The Lord doesn't owe us any explanations, but He graciously reveals Himself and His work to those who seek Him."

In verses 14-17, Habakkuk wants to clarify what God is saying. It's as if he can't believe what he has heard. Habakkuk says, really God? These evil people? These people who only worship themselves and their weapons of war? How long must these people keep destroying us?

God is clear though. He cannot tolerate wrong. He will not let you continue to live in willful sin. Remember all the evil kings we learned about in the previous week? God's people have lived in willful sin for far too long. God has warned them and warned them and warned them. Look back to week 1, day 2: What 2 reasons did God give for allowing the Babylonians to invade Judah?

_____
_____
_____

The people of Judah now had to live with the consequences of their willful sin.

What willful sin is in your life?

_____

Remember: God loves you too much to allow you to stay in sin. He is in the business of restoration.

Day 5: Your Honesty to God and God's Honesty to You

§

YOUR HONESTY TO GOD

WE HAVE JUST LEARNED THAT God has spoken some hard truths to Habakkuk about the future. God has revealed to Habakkuk that the evil Babylonians will conquer the Israelites.

God has even revealed His reason why. He loves His people too much to see them kept in the sin of idolatry and breaking the Sabbath.

God and Habakkuk had a completely honest and unfiltered conversation. Habakkuk first approached God with his problem with the ungodly people of Judah. Then when he learns of God's plans, he approached God with the question of why God chose to use the despicable Babylonians to punish the people of Judah.

Don't miss the fact that Habakkuk immediately went to God with his problems, concerns, and questions. When problems, concerns or questions arise in your life - where do you go to first:

A) friends or family
B) social media

C) keep it to yourself and withdraw from others
D) ignore the problem completely

James Montgomery Boice says in his book, "The Minor Prophets," "When we face problems it is important that we follow a proper procedure in dealing with them. When things go wrong, some people tend to withdraw. They drop out of Christian activities, stop going to church, pull back into their spiritual corner, and pout. Others repudiate their past. They conclude that they must have been wrong about God and renounce all belief in Him."

We can learn a lot from Habakkuk on the best way to handle our problems. Bring them immediately to God. God can handle our questions, concerns, doubts, fear, and emotions. He wants us to lay it all at His feet.

My husband Randy is a tell-it-like-it-is guy. He always speaks truth. I learned very early that if I ask him if my dress looks too tight, I better be prepared for the truth. He never sugar coats his words. In fact, the only thing he ever sugar coats is the frosting he makes for a cake.

God will also tell us like it is. He told me that enough was enough with my history of hurt. We have to be willing to give everything to God and let Him speak the truth to us.

Often God is the last person we approach. Jesus did not die on the cross so that we could handle our problems ourselves or spew them onto others. Jesus wants us to bring everything to Him first.

Boice continues to write, "You must say, 'Lord, I have done everything I know to do with this problem. I have faced it on the basis of everything I know, and I still don't understand it. From here on it's your problem, not mine anymore.' That is what God wants you to do. He wants you to make your problems His problems, because He knows that then you will grow in faith and your knowledge of Him will deepen. In time God will give you a proper answer to the problem you are facing."

Is there anything that you haven't brought to God? Bring it completely to Him now.

_____

_____

GOD'S HONESTY TO YOU

Our God is a God of Truth. The name El Emeth (El EH-met) means God of Truth.

Have you ever been lied to? Have you ever been told a story that you knew was a stretch of the truth? Have you taken someone's word for truth only to find out later that it was a lie?

Write a lie that someone told you that caused you great pain.

_____

_____

We have all had pain in our life that resulted from lies.
A lying spouse, a lying child, a lying friend, a lying boss, a lying co-worker, a lying sibling, a lying parent, a lying stranger. Lies can cause a lot of damage in our lives.

Write a lie that you told someone.

_____

_____

We live in a fallen world where lies constantly surround us. In a world filled with lies, half-truths, inconsistencies, stretches of the truth, distortions of truth and spins of words geared to our liking, it is hard to know what to believe.

However, there is one book that is only filled with truth and is crystal clear about lies in this world. It is God's word, the Holy Bible.

Read John 8:42-47. Who does the Bible say is the father of lies? _____. Does the father of lies have any truth in him? _____

If Satan is the father of lies, who is the Father of truth? _____

Fill in the blanks after reading:

Isaiah 65:16 "Whoever invokes a blessing in the land will do so by the _____ of _____, he who takes an oath in the land will swear by the _____ of _____. For the past troubles will be forgotten and hidden from my eyes."

Proverbs 30:5 "Every word of _____ is _____; He is a shield to those who take refuge in Him."

God is TRUTH

He is incapable of being anything else. It is impossible for Him to lie.

Our God is ALWAYS true to His word. He means what He says and says what He means. He's trustworthy, He's faithful, He's loving, He's consistent, He's just, He's detailed, He's concise.

If you have a tendency to not trust people or be skeptical of most people, you may find it difficult to trust God. However, he is the ONLY ONE that can be fully trusted. He speaks truth to us (even difficult truth). He lives TRUTH. He is TRUTH. His whole character is based on TRUTH. He is not a God that sugar coats the message. He has no hidden agenda. He is upfront and honest with His message to us.

Take a minute to really digest this. God can only speak truth. No lies will ever come from His mouth. EVER. His past is truth; His present is truth; His future is truth.

When we seek Him, we find truth.
When we call on Him, we find truth.
When we live for Him, we live in His truth.
When we listen to Him, we hear His truth.
All truth.
All the time.

His message of truth is unlike anything we see in our current society. In a world where everyone has a hidden agenda, greedy motives, passive aggressive tendencies, our God is so loving that He only wants our lives to work out for good.

God's history with His people has always had one message: Love me and keep my commands and I will take care of you and bless you.

Seek me and you will find me.
Keep my commands and you will be blessed.
Worship other gods and I'll turn away from you.

Even if the truth hurts, God does not hide it. He speaks truth to us even tough truth. The type of truth that we don't want to hear but need to hear. He does this to increase our faith in Him, to deepen our relationship with Him, to trust in His ways. He doesn't have anything to hide from us. Even in times when God tells us to wait and be patient, He does this for our good and future blessings.

We learned that God's truth to Habakkuk was a tough truth, a truth that Habakkuk did not expect nor understand.

Has there been a time in your life that God has given you a tough truth?

_____
_____

Was there a time when God spoke a truth to you that you completely did not understand?

_____
_____

God's T.R.U.T.H.: Truly Receiving Understanding Through Him

Day 1: Read and Receive

§

FOR TODAY, READ CHAPTER 3 in Stan's section. Make notes of the truths
that God wants you to receive from this writing.

_____

_____

_____

_____

_____

_____

_____

_____

_____

_____

_____

_____

Day 2: Habakkuk's Heart

§

WE HAVE LEARNED ABOUT HABAKKUK'S history. We have heard his honesty. Now we will feel his heart.

Even with God's unpleasant answers, Habakkuk CHOOSES to trust Him. Habakkuk's heart is aligned with God's heart.

Let's look at Habakkuk chapter 2, verse 1:
"I will stand at my watch and station myself on the ramparts; I will look to see what He will say to me, and what answer I am to give to this complaint."

During Habakkuk's time, the rampart was a protective barrier that overlooked the city to watch for the invasion of enemies.

Notice Habakkuk's resolve - he doesn't say that he should or he might; he says he will. He WILL stand and he WILL look. Habakkuk has been honest with God. He has heard from God. He has cleansed his heart before God. He now resolves to look and receive help from God.

Habakkuk is not trying to change God's mind. He's trying to change his own mind. He accepts God's will and is now ready to stand strong and commit his complete faith in Him. He says to God that he can't handle this problem himself. He has to rely on God for this problem. He has to wait on God in handling this problem. This is certainly not something that comes easily to us. Our flesh wants to do anything except wait. Waiting takes work. It's not a passive action.

Verse 1 can be translated - I will position myself close to you, Lord. I will not move away. While I wait on You, I will watch daily for what You want to say to me. I will stay strong. I will not give up.

Watching daily is like going on a God treasure hunt everyday. God wants us to be continually engaged with Him - actively pursuing His actions. It's our waking up every day and saying, "Good morning, God. I'm ready to receive what you have for me today. I'll be watching all day to see Your mighty hands at work."

My kids often hear me say aloud, "Good morning, God." My oldest son likes to remind me that God never sleeps, is always awake and doesn't need to be told good morning. I say to him that is certainly true but God loves our cheerfulness and open communication to Him. God wants to know that we are alert for His actions. We are on a daily treasure hunt to find Him in every situation.

How can we stay strong in our waiting and watching? We have to live in the scriptures.

Look up the following verses and fill in the blanks:

Colossians 4:2 "Devote yourselves to prayer, being _____ and thankful."

Psalm 91:4 "He will cover you with his feathers, and under His wings you will find refuge; His faithfulness will be your shield and _____."

Proverbs 8:34 "Blessed is the man who listens to me, _____ _____ at my doors, _____ at my doorway."

Post these verses on your mirror in your car, in your prayer journal, and on your refrigerator. Memorize them and keep reminding yourself that God is working on your behalf even if you can't see anything yet. Keep watching!!!

Day 3: God's Heart

§

WE LEFT OFF YESTERDAY WITH Habakkuk's resolve to watch and wait for God's answer. In today's devotion, God answers him.

Habakkuk 2:1-3
"Then the Lord replied: 'Write down the revelation and make it plain on tablets so that a herald may run with it. For the revelation awaits an appointed time; it speaks of the end and will not prove false. Though it linger, wait for it; it will certainly come and will not delay.'"

Translation: Write down what I am saying because it is important for you as well as others. My answer will come at just the right time. My answer will be enough for now and the future. My answer will be all truth. Even though you will have to wait for my answer, it will come at the perfect time (not too soon and not too late).

Write down the revelation:
God wants us to write down the revelation. He asks this of us so we won't forget the revelation in the future and that the revelation will be shared with others. It was standard practice in the Old Testament times for the Israelites to mark the spot where a miracle had occurred. They did this so they (and their children) wouldn't forget God's faithfulness.

I love God's heart. He assures Habakkuk and us that He has the perfect answers that will be revealed at the perfect time. It's important to God that we not only receive His answers in faith but to share His answers with others.. Our relationship with the Lord is not to be hidden. Our God's greatness and faithfulness is for the whole world to know.

Write down a time that God gave you an answer to a request or a problem:

_____

_____

Did you share God's revelation with others? Why or why not?

_____

_____

God's faithfulness in answering our prayers, requests, and/or complaints should not be kept to ourselves. Share it with your spouse, your kids, your friends, your co-workers.

Wait for the revelation:
This is the hard part. God clearly tells us that His answer will be revealed to us at the perfect time - His perfect time, not ours. We want the answer now.

Why do you think God wants us to wait for His answers?

_____

One year our family had to make an important decision about school. Randy and I decided to introduce Habakkuk to our kids and use the verses to receive direction on God's will. At the time, our 2 oldest kids were part of a homeschool co-op. They attended traditional classes for

3 days a week and then we homeschooled for 2 days a week. The school days were great but our homeschool days were miserable. My relationship with my kids was deteriorating. I was not a good homeschool mom. My kids were not good homeschool kids. Things had to change. I didn't know God's will but I knew that He did not want us to remain in discouragement and defeat.

At the dinner table one night, Randy and I shared the story of Habakkuk and how he shared his heart with God and then resolved to wait and watch for God's answer. Our family made the commitment to pray the "Habakkuk prayer" daily:

"The Allston family will stand at our watch and station ourselves on the ramparts; we will look to see what the Lord will say to us and what answer we are to give to our school situation" (Adaption of Habakkuk 2:1).

The kids wanted to know how God would reveal His answer. Randy and I said that God will work in each of our hearts to bring us into a unified decision. We said that God would give daddy the decision first, then mommy, then the kids. We all agreed to not share our hearts until Randy and I felt God's peace and direction in the decision.

After 3 months of "Habakkuk prayers," we opened the discussion. We each took a turn in sharing what God was saying in our hearts. None of us had shared our thoughts before this. We were all in unanimous agreement that we should transfer to full time traditional school. God was faithful to work in each of our hearts and make His will clear. Our older 2 kids admitted that it was not the decision they wanted but they knew in their hearts that it was what God wanted. How amazing and faithful God is.

I encourage you to use the "Habakkuk prayer" for your life. Complete the prayer:

"I, _____, will stand at my watch and station my-self on the ramparts; I, _____, will look to see what He will say to me, and what answer I am to give to the following situation _____
_____
_____."

God's heart is ready to be shared with you at the right time. Until then, keep praying the above prayer and enjoy the God treasure hunt!

Day 4: Read and Receive

§

FOR TODAY, READ CHAPTER 4 in Stan's section. Make notes of the truths that God wants you to receive from this writing.

_____

_____

_____

_____

_____

_____

_____

_____

_____

_____

_____

_____

Day 5: Your Heart

§

WE HAVE FOUND HABAKKUK'S HEART. We have found God's heart.

Where is your heart?

Habakkuk 2:4 is a verse spoken from Habakkuk about the Babylonians: "See, he is puffed up; his desires are not upright - but the righteous will live by his faith."

This is also a verse for you and me. It is such an important verse that it is repeated in the New Testament three times. The apostle Paul quotes it in his writings in Romans 1:17 and Galatians 3:11. It is also mentioned in Hebrews 10:38. Let's look up these Godly truths and commit them to memory.

Romans 1:17 "For in the gospel a righteousness from God is _____, a righteousness that is by _____ from _____ to _____, just as it is written: 'the _____ will _____ by _____.'"

Galatians 3:11 "Clearly no one is _____ before God by the law, because, 'the _____ will _____ by _____.'"

Hebrews 10:35-38 "So do not throw away your _____;
it will be richly _____. You need to _____
so that when you have done the _____ of God, you will receive
what He has _____. For in just a very little while, 'He
who is coming will come and _____ _____ _____.
But my righteous one will _____ _____ _____. And if
he _____ back, I will not be _____ with him.'"

The righteous will live by his faith. Translation: Faith is a lifestyle -
not a switch to be turned on and off. Faith is an action verb. Our
hearts are to be full of faith no matter our emotions, feelings, circumstances, or thoughts.

Is our heart full of ourselves or full of faith in God?

James Montgomery Boice describes this verse in his book "The Minor
Prophets," "The way of the righteous is the way of faith in God. The
way of the wicked is the way of drawing back from faith in God. The
first submits to God and trusts God. The second submits to no one.
The person who chooses the second way is arrogant. He says, 'I don't
need religion. I can take care of myself. I can do without God.'"

Habakkuk was a prophet whose job was to share God's message with the
people - even when that message wasn't popular. He warned the people
of willful sins. God is also using Habakkuk's writings to warn us of the
dangers of only having faith in ourselves. Read Habakkuk 2:4-20.

Let's examine our hearts by looking at Habakkuk's warnings of woe:

1. Woe to the greedy (vs 6-8)
In what area of your life is greed above God? Have you confessed this
to God?

_____

_____

2. Woe to those who treat others unfairly (vs 9-11)
When was a time that you treated someone unfairly? Have you confessed this to God?

_____

_____

3. Woe to those who desire destruction and ill will toward others (vs 12-14)
The Babylonians used violence for destruction. Many of us today don't use violence but we do use revenge, negativity, gossip, aggressiveness, and humiliation to try to destroy those against us.
Is there revenge in your heart that needs to be confessed?

_____

_____

4. Woe to those who manipulate others for their own gain (vs 15-17)
The Babylonians would use alcohol to expose others for their own perversions.. Manipulation of others is a willful sin that can lead to heartache and destruction.
When was a time that you manipulated another person for your own gain? Have you confessed this to God?

_____

_____

5. Woe to those who put trust and faith in idols (vs 18-20)
Our God is not an image. He is living! Nothing and no one can give guidance like our living Lord.
What idol(s) have you put in front of God? Have you confessed this to God?

_____

_____

Our heart belongs to God and His heart belongs to you. What a gift!

Does your heart belong to God right now? Is your heart full of yourself or full of God? Ask God to make His heart your heart.

Let's examine our hearts by looking at Habakkuk's warnings of woe:

1. Woe to the greedy (vs 6-8)
In what area of your life is greed above God? Have you confessed this to God?

_____

_____

2. Woe to those who treat others unfairly (vs 9-11)
When was a time that you treated someone unfairly? Have you confessed this to God?

_____

_____

3. Woe to those who desire destruction and ill will toward others (vs 12-14)
The Babylonians used violence for destruction. Many of us today don't use violence but we do use revenge, negativity, gossip, aggressiveness, and humiliation to try to destroy those against us.
Is there revenge in your heart that needs to be confessed?

_____

_____

4. Woe to those who manipulate others for their own gain (vs 15-17)
The Babylonians would use alcohol to expose others for their own perversions.. Manipulation of others is a willful sin that can lead to heartache and destruction.

When was a time that you manipulated another person for your own gain? Have you confessed this to God?

_____

_____

5. Woe to those who put trust and faith in idols (vs 18-20)
Our God is not an image. He is living! Nothing and no one can give guidance like our living Lord.
What idol(s) have you put in front of God? Have you confessed this to God?

_____

_____

Our heart belongs to God and His heart belongs to you. What a gift!

Does your heart belong to God right now? Is your heart full of yourself or full of God? Ask God to make His heart your heart.

Day 1: Read and Receive

§

FOR TODAY, READ CHAPTER 5 in Stan's section. Make notes of the truths that God wants you to receive from this writing.

_____

_____

_____

_____

_____

_____

_____

_____

_____

_____

_____

_____

_____

Day 2: Habakkuk's Hope

§

WE HAVE BEEN WITH HABAKKUK on a long journey. Learning his history, hearing his honesty and feeling his heart. Today we will be inspired by his hope.

Look back at Habakkuk 1:2. What are his first four words?

_____ _____ _____ _____

Now look at Habakkuk 3:1-2. How are his words different from chapter 1?

_____

_____

Habakkuk has evolved from heartache to hope, from fear and frustration to faith, from pressure to praise

In chapter 1, Habakkuk was consumed with his circumstances. We will now see in chapter 3 that he is consumed with God - the best place we can ever be.

Habakkuk is now filled with hope, not because his circumstances have changed but because his perspective of God has changed. Habakkuk begins his conversation in this chapter with a prayer of praise: "Lord, I have heard of your fame; I stand in awe of your deeds, O Lord. Renew them in our day, in our time make them known; in wrath remember mercy."

His prayer is for all people to know of God's mighty works. We will look more closely at some of God's mighty works in tomorrow's devotion.

Let's fast forward to the latter part of verse 16 where Habakkuk resolves himself to God's will. "Yet I will wait patiently for the day of calamity to come on the nation invading us." This is a huge change from chapter 1 where Habakkuk is crying out to the Lord asking how long and why.

Habakkuk knows that calamity is still coming YET he chooses to keep his focus on God. Fill in the words from verses 17-18:

"_____ the fig tree does not _____ and there are no _____ on the _____, _____ the olive crop _____ and the fields produce no _____, _____ there are no sheep in the pen and no _____ in the stalls, _____ I _____ rejoice in the Lord, I _____ be joyful in _____ _____ _____."

Translation: THOUGH it looks like there is no hope and no future, YET I will still praise the giver of Hope and rejoice in my mighty God and Savior.

What is your *though and yet?*

Though I'm in a difficult circumstance with

_____

_____

Yet I'll praise my God and Savior by

_____

_____

So how did Habakkuk get to a prayer of praise during such difficult circumstances?
It was his resolve to let God control his mind and will. Look back at Habakkuk's words to God in these verses:

2:1 - I _____ stand; I _____ look
2:4 - the righteous _____ live by his faith
3:16 - I _____ wait patiently
3:18 - yet I _____ rejoice; I _____ be joyful

Yes, God, I WILL! I will stand; I will look; I will live by faith; I will wait; I will rejoice; I will be joyful. I will, I will, I will. These are more than words. This is a commitment to turn our thoughts away from circumstances and towards God.

We have to become a strong-willed child of God - A strong will to keep our eyes focused on our Savior instead of our circumstances. Take time now to put the following phrases on notecards that will help you reinforce your strong will.

I WILL STAND
I WILL LOOK
THE RIGHTEOUS WILL LIVE BY FAITH
I WILL WAIT PATIENTLY
I WILL REJOICE
I WILL BE JOYFUL

Day 3: God's Hope

§

WE LEARNED YESTERDAY THAT HABAKKUK's hope turned away from a change of circumstances to a strong will in God's greatness.

Today we will explore God's hope. What do you think is God's hope for you?

_____

_____

Habakkuk shows us in chapter 3 that God's hope is for His people to always remember His faithfulness to His people.

Habakkuk reminds himself (and us) of the many times that God delivered His people. These verses are a praise of remembrance. A praise of faithfulness. A praise for kept promises. Let's read these verses to better understand God's faithfulness.

In verse 3, Habakkuk remembers God revealing Himself to Moses and bringing the people out of captivity from Egypt (reference Exodus 12).

In verse 4, Habakkuk remembers God leading the Israelites in the wilderness (reference Numbers).

In verse 5, Habakkuk remembers God sending plagues on the Egyptians for not releasing His people (reference Exodus chapters 7-12).

In verse 7, Habakkuk remembers the enemies of God's people shrinking back in fear (reference Exodus 15:14-16).

In verses 8-9, Habakkuk remembers God parting the Red Sea to rescue His people from the Egyptians (reference Exodus 14:13-31).

In verse 10, Habakkuk remembers God using Deborah and Barak to lead His people away from their enemy (reference Judges 4:15; 5:21).

In verse 11, Habakkuk remembers God made the sun and moon stand still for Joshua to win his battle against the Amorites (reference Joshua 10:12-14).

In verse 14, Habakkuk remembers God using David to defeat the giant, Goliath (reference I Samuel 17:1-58).

Why do you think it's important for you to remember God's faithfulness?

_____

_____

By remembering His faithfulness, we can trust in His plans. His plans may not always be the plans that we want, but they are plans that will work for our good.

List 3 separate times that God was faithful in your life.

1.

_____

2.

_____

3.

_____

God's hope for His people has always been for them to trust Him and surrender their lives to Him. Through our surrender, He is always faithful to guide us in the way we need to go.

God's hope today is for each person to come willingly to Him through His son, Jesus Christ. Through God's son, Jesus, we receive eternal life in Heaven.. We also receive unconditional love, peace, righteousness, fulfilled promises, and faithfulness for our lives now on earth.

Fill in the blanks from Psalm 85:10-13
"_____ and _____
meet together; _____ and _____ kiss each other. _____ springs forth from the earth, and _____ looks down from heaven. The Lord will indeed give what is _____, and our land will yield its harvest. _____ goes before him and prepares the way for his steps."

What beautiful verses to remind us of God's hope for His people.

Day 4: Read and Receive

§

FOR TODAY, READ CHAPTER 6 in Stan's section. Make notes of the truths that God wants you to receive from this writing.

_____
_____
_____
_____
_____
_____
_____
_____
_____
_____
_____
_____
_____

Day 5: Your Hope

§

THIS IS OUR LAST DEVOTION day together. What a wonderful journey it has been. For many of you, this was your first time learning and studying Habakkuk.. I pray that you have gained much knowledge and insight into the life of God's prophet.

We don't know the rest of Habakkuk's story, but we do know that God was faithful in helping Habakkuk turn his focus to Him instead of the circumstances. We saw Habakkuk's perspective of God change before our eyes in these beautiful heart-felt chapters.

How has your perspective of God changed through this study and devotion?

_____

_____

Through Habakkuk's history, honesty, heart, and hope, we see a faithful God that holds him in every stage of his life. God is there to hold us too. Our God is a God of history. He is a God of honesty. He is a God of heart. He is a God of hope. He is YOUR God.

In these past devotion days, you have given God your history, honesty and heart. Now it is time to give God your hope. You have already answered what you think God's hope is for you. Now write down what your hope is with Him.

_____

_____

Let's look at Habakkuk's last verse in Chapter 3. Fill in the words.
"The _____ Lord is my _____;
He makes my _____ like the feet of a _____, He
_____ me to go on the _____."

What a beautiful ending to Habakkuk's writings. Habakkuk has come a long way from asking God why to praising Him for His strength. Not only is this verse a prayer for strength, it's also a prayer of praise. Habakkuk is praising God for the strength He will give. Habakkuk knows that with God's strength, he will overcome the Babylonian's invasion.

Habakkuk 3:19 has been a go-to verse for me for many years. It signifies that our God is always in control, always gives us a strong footing, and even gives us strength to do more than we could imagine.

While writing these devotions, there were many times that I became gripped with fear. I'm a speaker not a writer. Even though I knew God had called me to write this, I was filled with doubt and fear. That is often the point, isn't it? God calls us to do things that we are fearful of so that we can fully rely on Him. I prayed Habakkuk 3:19 many times to help me get through these writings.

Is there something that God is calling you to do that makes you fearful?

_____

_____

How can Habakkuk 3:19 help you to go on the new heights?

_____

_____

Use this verse as a prayer to use God's strength for whatever He is calling you to do. Also use this verse as a prayer of praise for God freely giving you the strength to do what He has called you to do.

Do you have a prayer of praise that you want to offer to the Lord for His faithfulness?

_____

_____

Just like Habakkuk, I pray that your journey will be moved from heartache to hope, from fear to faith, and from pressure to praise.

May God bless you and take you to the new heights!

BIBLIOGRAPHY

Armerding, C. E. *The Expositor's Bible Commentary, Volume 7, Haggai.* Edited by Frank E. Gaebelein, Grand Rapids, Michigan, Zondervan, 1985.

Baker, David W. *Nahum, Habakkuk, Zephaniah: An Introduction and Commentary.* Downers Grove, Illinois, Inter-Varsity Press, 1998.

Barker, Kenneth L., and Donald W. Burdick. *Zondervan NIV Study Bible: New International Version.* Grand Rapids, MI: Zondervan, 2002. Print.

Barker, Kenneth L., and Waylon Bailey. *Micah, Nahum, Habakkuk, Zephaniah.* Broadman and Holman Publishers, 1988.

Berkhof, Louis. *History of Christian Doctrines - Louis Berkhof - Paperback.* Grand Rapids, Revel, a division of Baker Publishing Group, 31 Dec. 1978.

Blue, Ronald J., et al. *The Bible Knowledge Commentary.* Wheaton, IL, Cook, David C., 31 Dec. 2003.

Boice, James Montgomery. The Minor Prophets. Vol. 2. 2 vols. Grand Rapids: Baker, 2006.

Carson, Donald A., *How Long O Lord*. Grand Rapids, MI, Baker Academic, Division of Baker Publishing Group, January 2007.

Constable, Thomas L. *Notes on Habakkuk, Nahum, Zechariah*. Sonic Light, 2015.

Erickson, Millard J. *Christian Theology*. 3rd ed., Grand Rapids, MI, Baker Academic, Division of Baker Publishing Group, 1 Aug. 2013.

Freeman, Hobart E. *An Introduction to the Old Testament Prophets*. Chicago, Moody Press, 1 Dec. 1968.

Grudem, Wayne, and Zondervan Publishing House. *Systematic Theology: An Introduction to Biblical Doctrine*. Grand Rapids, MI, Zondervan, 1 May 2002.

Harrison, R. K. *Introduction to the Old Testament*. Peabody, MA, Hendrickson Publishers, 1 Mar. 2004.

Johnson, Jan. *Habakkuk: Staying Sane in a Crazy World (the Truthseed Series)*. *Amazon.Com: Books*, Victor Books, July 1995, https://www. amazon.com/Habakkuk-Staying- Crazy- World- Truthseed/ dp/1564762572. Accessed 12 Oct. 2016.

Linden, David H. "Www.Grebeweb.Com/linden/habakkuk/Habakkuk_ 1-3.Doc." *David Linden's Theology Papers*, https://www.google.com/?gws_ rd=ssl#q=david+h+linden+habakkuk. Accessed 12 Oct. 2016.

MacArthur, John. *The MacArthur Study Bible: New King James version*. Nashville: Word Bibles, 1997. Web.

McGee, Vernon J. *Thru the Bible Commentary: Nahum Habakkuk 30*. Nashville, TN, Nelson, Thomas, 17 Feb. 1997.

Oden, Thomas C. *The Living God: Systematic Theology, Vol 1.* San Francisco, CA, Harper: San Francisco, 30 Sept. 1999.

Packer, J. I. *Knowing God.* 20th ed., Downers Grove, IL, United States, Inter-Varsity Press, US, 1993.

Pusey, E. B. *The Minor Prophets: A Commentary Explanatory and Practical.* Baker Book House, 1950, https://www.google.com/?gws_rd=ssl. Accessed 15 Oct. 2016.

Roberts, J. J. M. *Nahum, Habakkuk, and Zephaniah: A Commentary (Old Testament Library).* Louisville, KY, Westminster/John Knox Press, U.S., 1 May 1991.

Robinson, George L. *The Twelve Minor Prophets.* Grand Rapids, Baker Book House, 1976.

Stuhlmueller, Carroll, and Palmer O. Robertson. *Rebuilding with Hope: A Commentary on the Books of Haggai and Zechariah.* Grand Rapids, William B Eerdmans Publishing Co, 1 Dec. 1991.

Sproul, R. C., and Keith A. Mathison. *The Reformation Study Bible: English Standard version, containing the Old and New Testaments.* Orlando, FL: Ligonier Ministries, 2005. Print.

Wegner, Paul D. *ESV Study Bible.* Edited by Lane T. Dennis, ESV Text Edition 2007 ed., United States, Crossway Bibles, 15 Jan. 2012.

Wiersbe, Warren W. *Be Amazed (Minor Prophets): Restoring an Attitude of Wonder and Worship.* David C. Cook, Colorado Springs, CO, 2010.